THE STATE OF THE WORLD'S CHILDREN
1982–83

1/21/83.

2

THE STATE
OF THE WORLD'S
CHILDREN
1982–83

James P. Grant
Executive Director of the
United Nations Children's Fund
(UNICEF)

PUBLISHED FOR UNICEF
Oxford University Press

Oxford University Press, Walton Street, Oxford OX2 6DP
London Glasgow New York Toronto
Delhi Bombay Calcutta Madras Karachi
Kuala Lumpur Singapore Hong Kong Tokyo
Nairobi Dar es Salaam Cape Town
Melbourne Auckland
and associates in
Beirut Berlin Ibadan Mexico City Nicosia

Published in the United States by
Oxford University Press, New York
© *United Nations Children's Fund 1982*

ISBN 0 19 828464 0

Cover: Concept Graphic, Shipston-on-Stour, UK
Typesetting: Kylin typesetting, Oxford, UK
Design: PGT Graphic Design, Oxford, UK
Printed by: Underhills, Plymouth, UK.

UNICEF, 866 U.N. Plaza, New York, N.Y. 10017 U.S.A.
UNICEF Palais des Nations, CH1211 – Genève 10 – Suisse.

Foreword

This is the third annual 'State of the World's Children' report issued by James P. Grant, Executive Director of UNICEF.

Synthesising the experience of UNICEF's own work in over one hundred countries, as well as the views of leading international specialists, this year's report suggests that recent scientific and social breakthroughs have put into our hands the means to bring about a revolution in the health and well-being of the developing world's children. Given the will, it should now be possible to reduce child malnutrition and child deaths in the developing world by at least half before the end of this century — despite the dark economic times through which the world is now passing.

In making such breakthroughs relevant to the needs of the majority, the report emphasises that advances in social organization and people's participation are as important as technological innovation itself. And to illustrate the complex reality of that decentralised process, this year's 'Ideas in Action' report (Part II) tells the story of one community organization now being built — on the foundations of its own culture and traditions — in over seven hundred villages in Upper Volta. Written by Peter Adamson and seen through the eyes of two individual village people, 'The Rains' draws its characters and content from research undertaken in Yatenga Province during the early rains of 1982.

Finally, a statistical annexe brings together the latest United Nations figures on children and world development.

About the Authors

James Grant, an American citizen, was born in China in 1922. After graduating from Berkeley in 1943, he returned to China first in the armed forces and then for three years working in relief and development programmes. In 1951 he took a doctorate in Jurisprudence from Harvard and subsequently worked on American aid programmes in South Asia, becoming Director of the US aid mission to Sri Lanka. Returning to Washington, he became Deputy to the Director of the International Cooperation Administration, a predecessor of today's USAID, and, subsequently, Deputy Assistant Secretary of State for Near East and South Asian Affairs. From 1964 to 1967 he served as Director of the AID programme in Turkey, with the personal rank of Minister, and from 1967 to 1969 as an Assistant Administrator of AID. In 1969 he became President and Chief Executive of the Overseas Development Council, where he served for eleven years and made many important contributions to international development strategy. He took up his present appointment as the third Executive Director of the United Nations Children's Fund (UNICEF) in January 1980. James Grant is also President of the Society for International Development.

Peter Adamson was born in England in 1946. After graduating from Oxford University he became founder editor of the New Internationalist magazine which has recently been awarded the 1981 United Nations Association Media Peace Prize and the 1981 Paul G. Hoffman Award for its work in the field of world development. In recent years, as well as writing on development issues for national newspapers in many countries, he has also worked closely with BBC Television on documentary programmes about world development.

Contents

PART I

The State of the World's Children
by James P. Grant

PART II

Ideas in Action
by Peter Adamson

ANNEXE

PART I
THE STATE OF THE WORLD'S CHILDREN
1982–83

New Hope in Dark Times

IF THE WORLD'S political leaders were to walk together through a village in the developing world they would only recognise about 2 per cent of the child malnutrition all around them. Indeed so invisible is the problem that, in one recent study, almost 60 per cent of mothers whose children were suffering from malnutrition believed that their children were growing normally and developing well.

The Third World's hunger is a hidden hunger. Visible malnutrition is rare. And it is time that the skin and bone image of the starving baby — an image which is too often used to represent the developing countries — was replaced by a greater international understanding of what child malnutrition really means.

Today, an invisible malnutrition touches the lives of approximately one quarter of the developing world's young children. It quietly steals away their energy; it gently restrains their growth; it gradually lowers their resistance. And in both cause and consequence it is inextricably interlocked with the illnesses and infections which both sharpen, and are sharpened by, malnutrition itself. Perhaps as many as half of all cases of severe child malnutrition, for example, are precipitated not primarily by the lack of food but by intestinal parasites, fever and infection — especially diarrhoeal infection — which depresses the appetite, burns the energy, and drains away the body-weight of the child.

3

The net result is that every day of this last year more than 40,000 young children have died from malnutrition and infection. And for every one who has died, six now live on in a hunger and ill-health which will be for ever etched upon their lives.

No statistic can express what it is to see even one child die in such a way; to see a mother sitting hour after anxious hour leaning her child's body against her own; to see the child's head turn on limbs which are unnaturally still, stiller than in sleep; to want to stop even that small movement because it is so obvious that there is so little energy left inside the child's life; to see the living pink at the roof of the child's mouth in shocking contrast to the already dead-looking greyness of the skin, the colours of its life and death; to see the uncomprehending panic in eyes which are still the clear and lucid eyes of a child; and then to know, in one endless moment, that life has gone.

To allow 40,000 children to die like this every day is unconscionable in a world which has mastered the means of preventing it. Yet progress towards preserving the lives of our children is now actually slowing down. Between the end of World War II and the beginning of the 1970s, for example, child death rates in the low-income countries were reduced by half. Yet in recent year's that progress has not been maintained. And for many of the children in the developing countries, particularly in Africa and in the poorest urban neighbourhoods of Asia and Latin America, the quality of life has actually begun to fall as the economic foothold of their parents begins to crumble.

Overall, present trends predict that the proportion of the world's children who live without adequate food, water, health-care, and education — a proportion which has been steadily declining for more than a generation — will now

4

remain approximately the same at the end of this century as it is today. Meanwhile, the absolute number of children living and growing in malnutrition and ill-health is set to increase. According to the UN's Food and Agriculture Organisation, for example, a continuation of present trends until the year 2000 would see 'a horrifying increase in the numbers of the seriously undernourished to some 600–650 millions.' In other words, the number of malnourished children in the world would increase by approximately 30 per cent.

In response to this slowing down of progress, last year's 'State of the World's Children' report launched a discussion of the possible ways in which the development effort might maintain its momentum by building on the achievements and drawing on the lessons of recent years in order to find new ways of extracting more progress from every available dollar.

In particular, the report pointed to the potential inherent in peoples' participation and community organisation among the poor themselves; in the training of paraprofessional development workers to work with those communities to create basic services; and in the mutually reinforcing ties between health-care, water-supply, nutrition and education which, if properly understood and intelligently managed, can sharply increase the ratio between resources and results.

This year, in response to a clearly worsening position for the world's children, there is an even more urgent need to search the recent past for ways of streamlining our efforts in order to maintain progress for children even against the headwind of world recession.

To this end, UNICEF in recent months has been distilling down the lessons of its own 36-year effort to improve the lives of the world's children. At the same

5

time, we have also been consulting with colleagues in the United Nations family and with outside experts of standing and practical experience in the fields of child health and nutrition. And our overall conclusion from these deliberations is that, as has happened so often in human history, the deepening of the present crisis is now being matched by the arising of new opportunities on an equal if not greater scale.

So much so that UNICEF is now of the belief that the social and scientific breakthroughs of recent years are at this point coming together to put into our hands the sudden means of bringing about a revolution in child health. A serious commitment to that revoluttion by peoples and governments could yet re-accelerate progress for the world's children, slow down the rate of population growth, and reduce child malnutrition and child deaths by at least half before the end of the 1990s. In short, we believe that there is new hope in dark times.

A Children's Revolution

The backdrop to the children's revolution which we now believe to be possible is the idea that organised communities and trained paraprofessional development workers, backed by government services and international assistance, could bring basic education, primary health care, cleaner water and safer sanitation, to the vast majority of poor communities in the developing world.

Such strategies are now beginning to take hold in nations containing a majority of the developing world's population. At the same time, new scientific and technological breakthroughs have also been made against some of the most widespread and intractable problems of

6

health and nutrition. Put together, these social and scientific advances now offer vital new opportunities, four of which are described below, for improving the nutrition and health of the world's children. For all four actions, the cost of the supplies and technology would be no more than a few dollars per child. Yet they could mean that literally hundreds of millions of young lives would be healthier. And within a decade, they could be saving the lives of 20,000 children each day. It is not the possibility of this kind of progress that is now in question. It is its priority.

Oral rehydration therapy

The first breakthrough is the discovery of oral rehydration therapy (ORT). And its importance is that it can stop the dehydration — caused by the draining of the child's body as a result of diarrhoeal infection — which now kills an estimated 5 million young children a year and is by far the biggest single cause of death among the developing world's children.

Shortage of clean water, infrequent washing of hands, unsafe sanitation, and the lack of health education mean that the average child in a poor community of the developing world will have anything between six and sixteen bouts of diarrhoeal infection each year. Often the mother's response is to withhold food and fluid. And the result is that the child is malnourished by both the illness and the treatment. Each episode of the infection can increase malnutrition. Each increase in malnutrition increases the risk of another infection. Each period of weight loss, broken only by the plateaux of partial recovery, leads the child further down the broad staircase of malnutrition.

7

Most children recover. But many fall into sudden and severe dehydration. In only two or three days, 15 per cent of body-weight can be lost. And at that point, death is between one and two hours away.

This is not a theory. It kills a child every six seconds. And previously it could only be treated by qualified nurses or doctors using expensive intravenous feeding in an often inaccessible hospital. With the discovery of oral rehydration therapy, it can be treated by a mother giving her child the right mix of sugar, salt and water in her own home.

It is a breakthrough which was made possible by the discovery that adding glucose to a solution of salt and water can increase the body's rate of absorption of the fluid by 2500 per cent. But because it is also a breakthrough which could save the lives of up to 13,000 children every day, it has been described by *The Lancet*, a leading British medical journal, as 'potentially the most important medical advance this century.'

To realise the potential of the ORT breakthrough, there will have to be an equivalent 'social breakthrough' in making the knowledge and the means of oral rehydration therapy available to the 500 million mothers and young children in the poorest areas of the developing world.

To achieve that, every available channel will have to be involved — the community's own organizations, the radio and the mass media, the billboards and the adult education centres, the women's groups and the community development workers, the primary health care networks and the health services themselves.

In some communities oral rehydration salts can be made up in packets, ready to be dissolved in water, and sold for between 10 and 20 cents in the small stores and kiosks which are to be found in almost every rural village or urban neighbourhood of the developing world. In others, community development workers can advise mothers on how to make up their own salts using eight teaspoonfulls of sugar to one of salt per litre of boiled and cooled water.*

With the right ingredients available, and with the knowledge that drinking — not the withholding of fluid — is the right response to childhood diarrhoea, ORT could become a 'people's medicine' and put into the hands of parents themselves the means to save the lives of most of those five million infants who die each year from diarrhoeal infections.

UNICEF itself is heavily involved in this task of making ORT available across the developing world. In Nicaragua this year for example, we have helped to equip almost three hundred oral rehydration units serving over 155,000 children; to train more than 1,400 people to teach the use of oral rehydration salts; and to produce more than a quarter of a million leaflets explaining the treatment to mothers. Health volunteers — one for every 25 households — are helping to carry the message about ORT as a cure, and about clean water and frequent hand-washing as a prevention, for the diarrhoeal infections which now kill approximately 10 per cent of the nation's infants.

In Haiti, where diarrhoeal infection alone kills 130 out of every 1,000 children born in the shanty towns of Port-au-Prince, a nationwide campaign to promote the use of ORT is about to begin — backed by UNICEF, WHO, and the Pan American Health Organization. The aim is to

---

Too little sugar or none at all means that the salt and water solution will almost all pass straight through the child's body and there will be no rehydration. The addition of the right quantity of sugar dramatically increases absorption of the fluid. Too much sugar, and the absorption rate again decreases sharply.

9

save the lives of 10,000 children a year by 1987 — and to prevent the malnutrition of an even larger number.

In Bangladesh during the last year, half a million mothers have been taught how to make and use oral rehydration salts — and follow-up surveys have shown that 99 per cent of them are now able to make a safe rehydration solution for their children.

In Narangwal, India, the death rate among children aged between eight days and three years has already been halved by community development workers using just oral rehydration salts and penicillin.

This is ORT in practice. Carried through by committed governments, such a breakthrough would alone be enough to re-accelerate the world's flagging progress against child malnutrition and child deaths.

The need for ORT is clear. the technology is known. the means of dissemination are available. The receptiveness of parents has been demonstrated. The cost is small. And only an inexcusable lack of national and international will can now prevent the bringing of its benefits to the vast majority of children in need.

Universal child immunization

The second element of the childrens' revolution which is now possible is the increasing feasibility of immunizing all children against measles, diphtheria, tetanus, whooping cough, poliomyelitis, and tuberculosis, as long urged by WHO. Together, these six diseases kill an estimated 5 million children a year in the developing world and account for approximately one third of all child deaths. Tetanus alone kills a million children a year. Whooping cough claims the lives of another 600,000.

The need to administer repeated booster immuniza-

10

tions, to children, and the primary injection of newborns, requires a well-organised delivery system. Social breakthroughs in the organisation of communities, to ready them for immunisation campaigns, are therefore as important as the technology of immunisation itself.

In recent years, the growth of community organizations and the increase in the numbers of paraprofessional development workers has made the social organization of immunization more possible than ever before. To match these new developments, scientific advances have been made in producing vaccines which are more heat-stable and therefore more portable.

The sensitivity to heat of several vaccines has constituted one of the main constraints to the expansion of immunization programmes.

But work is now underway on the development of more stable and more effective vaccines and already major improvements have been made. Measles vaccine, for example can now be carried on patrol to reach rural populations further away from centres with refrigeration facilities.

The cost of immunizing a child has also decreased. Measles vaccine, as one instance now costs less than 10 cents per dose. And as with each of these possible interventions, the improvement of children's lives is as dramatic as the prevention of children's deaths. For such diseases are also major causes of malnutrition. Whooping cough, for example, can induce malnutrition by the frequent vomiting which its coughing fits provoke. Measles itself claims ten percent of the body weight in a quarter of all cases — and halts weight-gain for several weeks. And incomplete as it would be, immunization of all children against the major diseases would also be an indirect 'immunization' against malnutrition itself.

Any increase in protection against malnutrition would, in its turn, reduce the risk of infection. A malnourished child who contracts measles, for example, is approximately 400 times more likely to die of the disease than a child who is adequately fed.

The promotion of breastfeeding

The third low-cost opportunity to significantly accelerate progress in the nutrition and survival of infants is the campaign to halt and reverse the disastrous trend from breast to bottle-feeding. And if such a campaign were comprehensive enough to change medical attitudes and hospital practices, to control irresponsible promotion and marketing of artificial infant formulas, and to help mothers both to improve their own nutrition and to be reassured that breastfeeding is best, then UNICEF believes that one million infant lives a year could be being saved within a decade from now.

It is a campaign to which UNICEF, the World Health Organization, and many other individuals and organizations are now committed. And the facts are these:

Breastmilk is the best food for a baby in any society. But in the materially-poor communities of the developing world, its advantages over bottle-feeding can widen to a difference between life and death.

Usually unable to read the instructions on a tin of formula, or to afford enough artificial milk over so many months, or to boil water every four hours, or to sterilize the necessary equipment, or to return to breastfeeding once she has stopped, the low-income mother who is persuaded to abandon breastfeeding for bottle-feeding in the developing world is being persuaded to spend a significant proportion of her small income in order to expose her child

12

to the risk of malnutrition, infection and an early grave.

The evidence to prove what common sense suggests has recently been coming in from all parts of the world. In Brazil a 1980 study found that among the young children of poor parents, bottle-fed babies were between three and four times more likely to be malnourished. In Egypt, a similar study of bottle-feeding has shown the risk of infant deaths to be five times greater. In Chile, WHO has reported that babies bottle-fed for the first three months of life were three or four times more likely to die than their brothers or sisters who had been exclusively breastfed. In India, bottle-fed babies have been found to suffer from twice as many respiratory infections and three times as many episodes of diarrhoea as babies who had been fed at the breast.

Perhaps most dramatic of all is the recently published evidence from a four-year UNICEF-sponsored study of over 10,000 new born babies in the Baguio General Hospital in the Philippines. Half way through that four year period, in the words of the Hospital's Chief of Pediatrics, Natividad Relucio-Clavano, 'I closed the door of the nursery to the milk companies. We stopped giving our babies the standard dose of infant formula. Down came the colourful posters and calendars. In their place, we hung the 'baby-killer' posters which show an emaciated baby inside a dirty feeding bottle. Everything that was conducive to bottle feeding was removed not only from the nurseries, but from everywhere else in the hospital. I myself rejected samples and donations from the milk companies.'

Over the next two years, among the new-borns of Baguio General Hospital, there was a precipitous fall in the incidence of infection, diarrhoea, and death.

The advantages of breastmilk begin with improved

hygiene and nutrition but do not end there. In recent years, the immunological qualities of breast milk — and especially of the colostrum which precedes it — have been more fully appreciated. In addition, the prolactin which breast-feeding releases in the mother's own body is also a natural contraceptive. And although an unreliable form of family planning from the individual mother's point of view, it nevertheless prevents several million conceptions a year in mothers whose bodies have not fully receovered from a previous pregnancy.*

Finally, breastmilk is cheaper. The foreign exchange costs to the developing nations of imported baby milk formula will run into billions of unnecessary dollars in the 1980s. And for individual families, the cost of feeding a baby on adequate quantities of artificial milk works out at more than half of a labourer's weekly wage in Uganda, or Jamaica or Nigeria, or of a clerk's take-home pay in Sri Lanka or Indonesia. Not surprisingly, one recent study in Barbados found that three quarters of low-income families who had abandoned breastfeeding were stretching a four-day tin of baby milk to make it last anything between five days and three weeks. At that point of course, it is the infants themselves who pay the highest price.

In Brazil, the percentage of babies being breastfed has fallen from 96 per cent in 1940 to 40 per cent in 1974. In Chile, from 95 per cent in 1955 to 20 per cent today. In Mexico, from 95 per cent in 1960 to less than 40 per cent by 1966. In Singapore, from almost 80 per cent in 1951 to only 10 per cent in 1971. In the Philippines, from 63 per cent in 1958 to 43 per cent in 1968. In Rep. of Korea, from 55 per cent in 1950 to 35 per cent in 1970.**

Alan Berg, Senior Nutrition Adviser to the World Bank, has estimated that approximately five million births per year could be avoided in India alone if breastfeeding were 'effectively carried out.'

Among the main causes of that decline has been the spread of artificial infant milk whose manufacturers looked outward from the stagnating markets of the industrialized countries in the 1960s and 70s and saw the potential of increasing sales among the large and rising infant populations of the developing world. And to a mother whose confidence may already be low in the face of more 'scientific' ideas and more 'modern' products imported from other cultures, even the most innocent promotions — 'for those who can't breastfeed' or 'for mothers with insufficient milk' — can create the anxiety which is one of the major causes for breastfeeding's decline. In the words of Priyani Soysa, Professor of Paediatrics at the University of Colombo, 'it is the lack of self-confidence which undermines the possibility of successful lactation as well as the excessive anxiety over the baby's well-being which is creeping into the modern sectors of poor countries.'

In recent years, the fight back has begun. At least 35 nations have now adopted measures based on the 1981 World Health Assembly's 'International Code on the Marketing of Breastmilk Substitutes' and many manufacturers of infant formula have begun to change their marketing practices towards an accordance with the code.

The results are already reducing malnutrition and saving lives. In Papua New Guinea, where legislation was passed as early as 1977, the bottle-feeding of babies has fallen from 35 per cent to 12 per cent and the percentage of seriously under-nourished infants has also fallen from 11 per cent to four per cent.

In India, WHO and UNICEF have jointly sent letters

** *These figures are based on different ways of measuring the extent of breast-feeding in different countries. In industrialised countries breastfeeding, after a steep decline, is increasing again.*

to all members of parliament and all paediatricians explaining the campaign to promote breastfeeding and asking for their support. At the same time, UNICEF publications about breastfeeding — reinforced by advertisements in popular magazines —have now reached all medical and health institutions in the sub-continent. In Pakistan, in the Philippines, in Bangladesh, in Indonesia, in Afghanistan, in Sri Lanka, in Thailand, we are working with local organizations and opinion-leaders — as well as with health ministries — to incorporate the promotion of breastfeeding into adult education and primary health care. In Zimbabwe, booklets on the advantages of breastfeeding and the case for controlling the promotion of artificial infant food have been sent to 25,000 health workers. In the Arab world, and in co-operation with Arab media and governments, the benefits of breastfeeding have been promoted both to health and nutrition workers and to the general public. In the Caribbean, UNICEF has assisted nine nations to issue guidelines on breastfeeding to obstetricians and health workers throughout the region.

Not all the codes now being adopted are as effective as they should be. But a start has been made on a campaign in support of which governments and people the world over can help to reduce the most unnecessary malnutrition of all. That campaign has UNICEF's fullest moral and material support.

Growth charts

The fourth possible breakthrough against child malnutrition and ill-health is the mass use of simple cardboard child-growth charts kept by mothers in their own homes, as a stimulus and guide to the proper feeding of the pre-school child.

Almost all child malnutrition is invisible — even to mothers. Consistent under-nutrition, successive infections, and bouts of diarrhoeal disease, can all hold back a child's growth over weeks and months in a way that may pass unnoticed by the mother. But it will not pass unnoticed by the chart.

Regular monthly weighing, and the entering up of the results by the mother herself, can make malnutrition *visible* to the one person who cares most and can do most about improving the child's diet. And there is evidence to suggest that in as many as half of all cases of child malnutrition it is the invisibility of the problem, rather than the lack of food in the family, which is the principal constraint on improving the nutritional status of the child.

That is why the simple act of rendering the problem visible can in itself reduce the incidence and severity of child malnutrition. A child who has just had measles or suffered an episode of diarrhoea, for example, may well have failed to gain in weight from one monthly weighing to the next. When the mother can *see* that this has happened, her spontaneous reaction, if there is food available, is to give the child more at the family's evening meal, or to feed the child more frequently, or to persist in persuading and helping the child to eat even when appetite is depressed.

To take one specific example, the chart on page 18 (fig. 1) plots the growth of one individual child in a poor Central American community and tells a story which is typical of childhood in the developing world. For the first six months of life, breastfeeding keeps this infant growing normally. Thereafter, as weaning begins and contact with the outside world increases, malnutrition and infection, each making the other worse, begin to drag down the child's growth so that the weight gain between the ages of six months and three years is only 1.5 kilos.

17

Figure 1

The chart below plots the growth of an actual child in a poor Central American community and tells a story typical of the childhood of millions in the developing world. For the first six months of life, breastfeeding keeps the child growing normally. Thereafter, as weaning begins, malnutrition increases the risk of infection and infection exacerbates the malnutrition. Together, they attack the child's rate of growth so vigorously that there is no weight gain at all between the age of six months and eighteen months. Often, the flattening of the child's weight curve is a slow and invisible process — especially if it is also happening to a majority of the children in the community. But regular monthly weighing and the use of a simple growth chart — kept at home by the mother — is an early warning system which makes malnutrition visible and can be a vital aid to the mother in maintaining her child's growth and health.

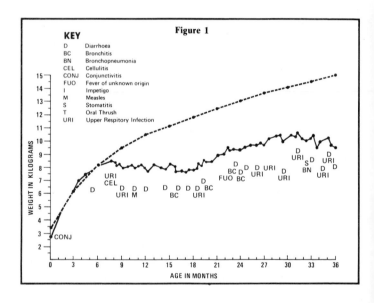

The chart shown here is based on studies by L.J. Mata, J.J. Urrutia, and A. Lechtig for the Institute of Nutrition of Central America and Panama (INCAP)

18

If the mother of this child had been able to see this problem — on a growth chart in her own home — then the child's progress would almost certainly have been better. Apart from being a scientific early-warning system, such charts can offer encouragement by making the solutions as visible as the problems. Breastfeeding's success, for example, is clearly visible on this chart. And immunization and the availability of oral rehydration therapy would both have made a dramatic difference to a child whose 'life-line' shows approximately 16 weight losses from diarrhoeas and infectious diseases in its first three years.

Often, growth charts have been kept in clinics rather than in homes and the weighing, monitoring and evaluating have been the responsibility of health personnel rather than of mothers. But the revolutionary potential of the growth chart will only be released when this pattern is reversed and the technology of the chart and scales is used to involve and *enable* the mother in the task of improving her child's nutrition rather than to alienate her from that responsibility by professionalizing the process and wrapping its techniques in mystery.

In Indonesia today, two million mothers in 15,000 villages are regularly weighing their babies at monthly village 'rallies' where the women hold their traditional get-togethers. The weighing scale used is the familiar market place 'dacin' on which illiterate mothers can measure their children's weight to within an accuracy of 50 grammes. Those who can read then help the illiterate to plot the result of the weighing on the mother's own growth chart.

Rather than comparing the child's growth curve to that of a 'normal' child — which is often unnecessarily worrying to the mother — the growth charts now being used in Indonesia concentrate on the child's own individual growth. And the main message conveyed is that a

19

rising line of monthly dots is good, a level line means more food is needed, and a falling line is a sign of danger, calling out for more food and perhaps medical attention. Around the edges of the chart, panels can carry details of the child's immunization record plus basic messages on improved child health — messages about breastfeeding, about oral rehydration, about hand-washing, or about suggested weaning food mixes.

After each weighing, the monitoring and evaluation — and the necessary action — is in the hands of the mother. 'By promoting do-able, home-based, self-financed activities as soon as growth falters' says Dr. Jon Rohde, one of the pioneers of the Indonesian experiment, 'growth can be achieved and normal nutritional status preserved even in the face of frequent illness or relative food shortage.'

During 1983, the first full evaluation of the experiment will be available and the potential of the charts will be more precisely known. But there is already some evidence that the number of cases of acute malnutrition has been significantly reduced since the charts began to be used. And similar campaigns are now moving forward, with UNICEF's support, in other parts of the developing world.

In other regions and cultures, the child growth chart idea would need to be assimilated into other familiar forms of weighing, other traditional forms of social organization, other opportunities for participation. In some places, the weighing itself may be the stimulus around which the means and the knowledge of other health improvements — information about oral rehydration salts and vaccination campaigns, discussion of weaning foods and breast-feeding, provision of iron and folate pills for pregnant women and of vitamin A tablets for children — might be made available. In other places, other activities might provide the forum for participation — and therefore the point of entry for the technology of growth charts to become what it ought to be — a people's science.

Social organization

These four specific opportunities — oral rehydration therapy, universal child immunization, the promotion of breastfeeding, and the mass use of child growth charts — are all low-cost, low-risk, low-resistance, peoples' health actions which do not depend on the economic and political changes which are necessary in the longer term if poverty itself is to be eradicated. They are therefore available *now.*

In practice, all four of these actions could help to stimulate further participation in further health improvements. Similarly, all four would be mutually reinforcing — so that the impact of the whole could be considerably greater than sum of the parts. Taken together as the leading edge of a basic services and primary health care strategy, and vigorously backed by governments and international agencies, UNICEF believes that these new opportunities have opened up the possibility of a children's revoution which could re-accelerate progress and save the lives of 20,000 children each day by the end of the 1990s.*

This opportunity to do so much for so many and for so little comes at a crucial moment in history. It holds out hope for children in darkening times. And it arises as much from social as from technical change. Fifteen years ago, for example, such a revolution would not have been

---

* *It should be stressed that these four actions are not the only possibilities. There are other priority health problems such as intestinal parasites, malaria, upper respiratory infections, and low birth weight, for which low-cost measures are also available. The precise mix of appropriate activities needs to be decided in response to local problems.*

possible. Social organization is the key to community health. And in recent years, the patient work of communities, individuals, government bodies, non-governmental organizations, and international agencies, has helped both to discover these new opportunities and to help create the growing social infrastructure — the community organizations and the paraprofessional development workers, the primary schools and the primary health networks, the peoples' movements and the trained professionals, the roads and the radios — which now make such revolutionary progress possible.

In Asia alone, for example, India has trained 100,000 community health workers and retrained 150,000 traditional birth attendants in recent years. In Thailand, 11,000 village health workers have been given basic training and 112,000 'village health communicators' are now serving almost a quarter of the population. In Vietnam, 8,500 health centres support the work of community development workers selected and paid for by each community. In China, over two million 'barefoot doctors', are providing basic health care — backed by highly sophisticated services where necessary — for a billion people. And in the last year alone, nearly 900,000 people have received training or re-orientation through UNICEF stipends and more than 300,000 institutions — from primary schools to village health centres — have received UNICEF supplies and equipment.

These 'social breakthroughs' are the missing link between the know-how of science and the needs of people. And where that link is in place, a sudden increase in child health and child survival is now clearly possible.

Birth spacing

At this point, an obvious question arises from the

22

apparent conflict between this potential 'survival revolution' and the need of the majority of developing countries to slow down their rates of population growth. But it is a conflict which is dissolved by time. For when people become more confident that their existing children will survive, they tend to have fewer births. That is the principal reason why no nation has ever seen a significant and sustained fall in its birth rate without first seeing a fall in its child death rate.

Historically, when overall death rates make that first steep fall from around 40 per 1,000 as a result of eliminating epidemics, the decline in birth-rates follows a long way behind. The result is rapid population growth. Fortunately, history has also shown, in the era since World War II, that when overall death rates have fallen to around 15 per 1,000 people — which, significantly, is about the average for the low-income developing countries today — then each further fall of one point in the death rate has usually been accompanied by an even larger fall in the birth rate. Thailand's 7 point fall in death rate (15 to 8 per 1,000) between 1960 and 1980, was accompanied by a 14 point fall in the birth-rate. In the same period, Costa Rica's 5 point fall in death rate (10 to 5 per 1,000) was accompanied by an 18 point fall in the birth-rate. Similarly, an 8 point fall in the death rate of the Philippines was accompanied by a 12 point fall in birth-rates.

Paradoxically, therefore, a 'survival revolution' which halved the infant and child mortality rate of the developing world and prevented the deaths of six or seven million infants each year by the end of the century, would also be likely to prevent between 12 and 20 million births each year.

The availability of family planning can shorten the time-lag between falling death-rates and falling birth-rates. But even if population growth were not a cause for concern, the availability of family planning would in itself have a crucial part to play in improving the health of mothers and children and reducing the rate of infant mortality. For too many births too close together undermine the health and the nutritional well-being of both mothers and children. A survey of 6,000 women in South India, for example, showed that the death-rate among infants born within one year of each other was approximately 200 per 1,000 as opposed to 80 per 1,000 among babies born three or four years apart. So making family planning widely available, although culturally and practically more difficult than the other specific interventions discussed earlier, is also one of the most important single steps which can now be taken towards reducing infant mortality and increasing the health of both mothers and children.

Political will

Even if the technological know-how and the social organization is available, re-accelerating progress in child health depends upon the will to do so. In some nations, political will can be stimulated by national and international advocacy. Research and publicity, for example, can help to get across the message that simple diarrhoea is the major killer of children in most countries of the world today and that a government committed to the greatest health of the greatest number at the lowest possible cost would certainly give more priority to oral rehydration salts than to heart-transplant technology.

But just as the political commitment — in support of technological and social change — can achieve results, so achieving results can help to bring about that commitment. For no advocacy is as convincing to governments as

24

successful action to demonstrate that substantial improvement is possible at low cost and in a short space of time. And one of UNICEF's goals, in co-operation with its many partners in the development process, is to demonstrate that potential.

But 'results' in reducing child malnutrition and child death rates will not look very impressive, at least in the short-term, if they are measured only by how much they contribute to increases in the Gross National Product. And another essential part of advocacy and action for re-accelerated progress in child health is a means of measuring what is being done by the yardstick of what is being attempted.

Because it reflects such progress as education, water supply, health care, and nutrition, for both the mother and the child, UNICEF believes that the infant mortality rate — the number of the deaths before the age of one for every 1,000 live births — is one of the most sensitive of all indicators of progress for children. Another possible measure is the Physical Quality of Life Index (PQLI) which takes three elements — the rates of infant mortality, literacy, and life expectancy at age one — and puts each on a scale with a high of 100 (representing the highest which any country is expected to achieve by the year 2000) and a low of zero (representing the lowest rate prevailing anywhere in the world of 1950). The PQLI then gives equal weight to each of these indicators and averages them into a single measure of the physical well-being of a given population. When used alongside the more conventional measure of Gross National Product, the PQLI reveals the kinds of disparities which ought to help generate the political will — as a matter of national pride if nothing else — to do something about it. When taken together with per capita GNP, the use of social indicators — either the infant mortality rate alone or the composite PQLI index itself — reveals a much more three-dimensional picture of development in a given country than either economic or social indicators standing alone.

Brazil, for example, is almost five times richer than Sri Lanka when conventionally measured by the yardstick of income per head. Yet Brazil's rates of literacy, life expectancy, and infant mortality give it a PQLI rating of 65 whereas the people of Sri Lanka have a PQLI rating in the 80s. More positively, there are already several parts of the developing world — China, Rep. of Korea, and Kerala in South India, as well as Sri Lanka — which can take justifiable pride in having reduced their levels of infant mortality to well under half the average rate for the developing world as a whole while their incomes were still low. Measuring the progress of child survival and child health by such criteria might therefore also help in the creation of political will and therefore in fueling the process itself.

Two years ago, these basic social indicators used in the PQLI index were incorporated, for the first time, into the targets set by the International Development Strategy for the 1980s and adopted by the General Assembly of the United Nations. Specifically, that Strategy asked the nations of the world to accept the goal that by the year 2000 the rate of infant deaths in the developing countries should be reduced to 50 or less, that average life expectancy should be raised to 60 or more, and that every child should have at least the four years of primary school education necessary to acquire lasting literacy.

Since then, progress towards all *three* of those goals has almost certainly slowed and the prospects of reaching them in the 17 years between now and the end of the twentieth century are being dimmed by the dark economic times through which the world — and its children — are now passing.

But if the political will can be created, then the opportunities outlined in this report so far, opportunities which have been distilled from and are available through the social and scientific progress of recent years, can be the additional means by which people participate in revolutionizing their own children's health and re-accelerating the planet's progress toward the goals which the international community accepted only two short years ago.

Food and Jobs

The opportunities discussed so far are all ways of 'taking up the slack' created by recent social and scientific advances. And they are all ways which would help to reduce malnutrition by helping to improve the use of available food — both in its use by the child's body and in its allocation by the child's family.

But these improvements can only go so far before running into the hard rock of the malnutrition problem — the lack of food itself. For if a family cannot provide enough calories, proteins and vitamins for a child's growth and health, then growth charts will flag the need for food in vain and malnutrition will become inevitable. Today, approximately one third of families whose children are malnourished fall into this category: they are just too poor to fight it.

For those who simply do not have enough to eat, the long-term solution lies in having either the land with which to grow food or the jobs and the incomes with which to buy it. But as many as one-third of the Third World's labour force is now unemployed or under-employed.

27

In the forseeable future, and in the absence of changes in the world's economic structure to allow the developing world to expand the exports of its manufactures, industry is unlikely to create employment on a scale commensurate with the problem of poverty and food. And it is therefore again to the rural areas that the search for vastly increased employment opportunities must turn.

The adage that two problems add up to a solution offers one clue in that search. For the problems of how to grow more food and how to create more work could in fact be mutually resolving.

If land concentration and large-scale mechanisation are kept under control then high yielding varieties of seed, for example, can yield more *jobs* per acre as well as more food. The need for irrigation, fertilization, pesticides, weeding and straight-line sowing rather than broadcasting, can all add up to as much as 40 per cent more labour over the agricultural year. And because small farmers tend to plan more thoughtfully, sow more economically, irrigate and fertilize less wastefully, harvest more thoroughly, and store more carefully, the yields on small farms are almost always higher than on larger holdings. Increases in both employment *and* productivity can therefore be not only compatible but mutually reinforcing.

The productivity of small labour-intensive farms of less than five acres in India, for example, is 40 per cent higher per acre than on farms of 50 acres or more. In Thailand, two to four acre farms produce 60 per cent more rice per acre than farms of 120 acres or more. And in one World Bank study of five Latin American nations, small farms were found to be anything from three to fourteen times more productive than large estates.

Where land is plentiful and labour is expensive, as in the

United States, it can be efficient to mechanize farms on large landholdings. But when labour is relatively plentiful and land is scarce, as in most of Asia, the opposite 'mix' makes more sense. In the early 1970s, for example, Japan and America, were two of the most efficient agricultural nations in the world in productivity per acre. Yet Japan had achieved that efficiency with a high ratio of labour to land (87 workers per 100 acres) and the United States had achieved it with a low ratio (one worker per 100 acres).

In general, the labour-intensive route to efficiency is more appropriate in most of the developing world today — as the example of Northeast Asia has convincingly shown. The average farmer in China, Japan, Rep. of Korea, Taiwan, for example, produces far more food per acre of land than his counterpart in India or Pakistan. And the reason is that credit and marketing, training and technology, education and health services, are geared to the family with an average holding of approximately two acres. In the Punjab of India and Pakistan, by contrast, such services have been geared to the farms of 20 acres or more.

Greater equity could therefore increase the production and lower the price of food. But, even more important, it could increase the production of food *by* the poor *for* the poor. And in so doing it could begin to break down the walls which have been built up between agriculture and nutrition in so many countries of the world. And at this point, of course, a better-nourished work force would add a new twist to the upward spiral of increasing employment and increasing production.

In several regions where land reform has become a reality — and especially where it has been accompanied by increased access to credit, training, irrigation, technology and markets — it has convincingly demonstrated its potential for increasing productivity *and* reducing malnutrition through the provision of incomes. In the late 1940s and early 1950s, for example, China, Taiwan, Rep. of Korea and Japan all began to initiate land reforms which sowed the seeds of subsequent agricultural success and made a major contribution towards virtually eliminating malnutrition within one generation.

Much else needs to be done to marshall human resources against a resurgent hunger. In particular agricultural research, which has paid such rich dividends to large landowners in recent years, now needs to be re-oriented towards the problems of poorer and smaller farmers. At the moment, probably no more than 1 per cent of the world's research into food and agriculture is focused on the problems of the hungry. A breakthrough in the techniques of dry land farming for unirrigated lands, or in nitrogen fixation by which food grains might fix their own fertiliser from the air, or in improved techniques of cultivating 'poor peoples' crops' such as cassava or sorghum, or in accelerating the progress of photosynthesis by which plants convert the energy of the sun into food, might help to solve the hunger problem by bringing science to bear on the needs of the majority.

All these are areas of research which might bring increased food production by and for the poorer farmers of the world and their families. And that is a much more important consideration, in relation to eradicating world hunger, than is the problem of increasing overall production. The amount of extra grain needed to close the 'calorie gap' in the developing countries, for example, will be approximately 30 million tonnes a year by the end of the 1980s. And that is less than 2 per cent of present world production and less than 20 per cent of the amount of grain now fed to cattle in the northern hemisphere each year. In the FAO's word, the gap is 'miniscule'.

However important increasing production may be, it is clearly not the central problem. And the answer to hunger is therefore not ultimately technological. The problem is rather one of what crops are grown by whom on whose lands and for whose benefit. And the solution lies in political and economic change to allow the poor to both participate in, and benefit from, the increases in production which can most certainly be achieved.

One of the most difficult and necessary of those changes is land reform itself. Two-thirds of the 'poorest billion' live in the rural areas of the developing world. And for the majority, whether there is enough food to eat depends on whether they have access to land and the right to the fruits of their own labour.

Some will no doubt say that UNICEF should concern itself with children, not employment and land reform. But concern for children cannot be oblivious to the fact that the death rate of those children in the villages of Bangladesh, for example, is twice as high in the families of the landless as in the families of those who own land; or that children in Costa Rica are significantly more likely to be malnourished if their families own less than one and a half hectares of land; or that the children of the landless in Guatemala are twice as likely to be malnourished as the children of those who own even three and a half acres of land.

Concern for children's health and nutrition is therefore inseparable from a concern over the lengthening shadow of landlessness cast by the increasing concentration of its ownership. In Bangladesh, for example, more than half the land is now owned by 10 per cent of the landowners. In the Philippines, four per cent of farms cover over a third of the country's cropland. In Kenya, 3,000 large farmers own more land than the country's three quarters of a million smallholders. In Bihar, India, the poorest half of the population has less than four per cent of the land. In Latin America as a whole, seven per cent of the landowners control 93 per cent of the soil whilst the poorest third of the people have to manage on just one per cent.

In total, an estimated 600 million people in the rural areas of the developing world now lack secure access to the land on which they could grow the food to feed themselves and their families. And as the ranks of the landless swell, those who oppose justifiable land reforms which could give millions of poor people in the world the means of producing food, may eventually prove the wisdom of the words that 'those who make peaceful change impossible make violent change inevitable'. Or as Pope John Paul II has expressed it 'the depressed rural worker, who with his sweat waters his affliction, cannot wait any longer for the recognition of his dignity. He has the right to be respected and not deprived with manoeuvres which are sometimes tantamount to real spoilation of the little he has. He has the right to be rid of the barriers of exploitation, often made up of intolerable selfishness against which his best efforts of advancement are shattered.'

Food supplements

Land reforms and economic growth to give the poor access to land, jobs, increased productivity, higher incomes, are an essential part of the long-term solution to the poverty from which malnutrition and ill-health are born. But for the very poorest families, hunger and ill-health themselves form a prison in which increased education, energy, and incomes are only to be gazed at through the bars. In many parts of Africa for example, and in the shanty towns which surround many of the Third World's cities, the poorest families are already spending three-quarters or more of their income on food and still they cannot keep malnutrition away from their children. And in many of those urban areas, food prices are likely to go on rising.

For such families, action against malnutrition is a minimum precondition for, and not an incidental by-product of, their economic development.

If the children of those poorest families are allowed to grow up malnourished, then the cycle of ill-health, low energy, low productivity, low incomes and low level of financial and energy investment in improving family and community life will be perpetuated into a new generation.

Somewhere, somehow, this cycle must be broken into. And experience suggests that the answer to 'where', is in pregnancy, lactation, and weaning, and that the answer to 'how' lies in some form of food subsidy for the families of those who do not have the means to earn enough to buy the right amount of food in those vital years.

Intervention to get more food to undernourished pregnant women is almost certainly the most cost-effective single point at which to break into that cycle. For it is known that the nutritional well-being of the pregnant woman is the most decisive factor in the birth-weight of the baby — and that the birth-weight of the baby is the most decisive factor in its chances of survival. Low birth-weight babies (below 2,500 grammes) for example, are three times more likely to die in infancy than babies of normal weight at birth. And the result is that the 10 to 15 per cent of babies born with low birth weights now account for between 30 and 40 per cent of all infant deaths in the developing world.

Applying this knowledge could therefore have a revolutionary impact on maternal and child health. In Guatemala, for example, supplementary feeding for undernourished women in the last three months of pregnancy has been shown to have reduced the incidence of low birthweight babies by 75 per cent and associated infant deaths by 50 per cent. And it is difficult to think of any investment in human life and health which could possibly be more cost-effective.

After the birth of the child, the mother needs both the reserves built up during pregnancy and an adequate daily intake of food if she is to meet the new energy demands of breastfeeding and all the additional tasks of looking after an infant's health and well-being. For the very poorest mothers at this time, some kind of food supplement is therefore again indispensible if the energy needs of mother and child are to be met.

At the age of five or six months, breastmilk alone is no longer sufficient for a child's needs. And if the gradual introduction of other foods does not now begin, then weight gain falters, the growth curve flattens, the risk of infection increases, and malnutrition takes a grip on the young child's life. Delaying weaning therefore gives millions of infants the first unintentional push down the slope of malnutrition. In India, for example, 36 per cent of all infants in the rural areas and 40 per cent among the urban poor are still being exclusively breastfed at the age of one year. For one-fifth of those children, weaning has not begun even at the age of eighteen months.

Regular monthly weighing and the use of growth charts is by far the best way for a mother to decide when weaning should begin. And immunization and oral rehydration therapy can help to combat the increased risks of infection and diarrhoea which come when a child is weaned into

34

more contact with food and water from the outside world. But it is just as important that the mother is able to give her child the right weaning foods in the right way and in the right quantities. And for that she needs both the knowledge — and the food.

During the vulnerable weaning period, nutrition education is therefore an important element of basic community services and primary health care. But it should not be forgotten that when the poorest mothers go shopping, they usually get two or three times more proteins and calories — per rupee — than the rich. Among the very poor, lack of income is therefore the main constraint on better diets. Subsidised food at the time of weaning, as well as in late pregnancy and early infancy, can therefore be the sharpest means of cutting into the closed circle of malnutrition which now traps the families of the very poor. And that food supplement might also be a necessary safety net for those families hit by drought or flood, or the desertion of a husband, or the loss of a job.

In sum, it does not seem likely that widespread malnutrition among the most needy families in the world can be effectively overcome without some form of consumer food subsidy, targeted to those most in need, in addition to the kinds of intervention outlined earlier in this report.

Food subsidy is a complex and controversial issue. But when the dust has settled, the fact remains that most nations which have ever made great progress in reducing malnutrition among the poorest of their peoples — from the People's Republic of China to the United States of America — have used food subsidies as one of the means of doing so. And its potential as a weapon against the worst of hunger has also been dramatically demonstrated in low-income developing nations like Sri Lanka, or in regions like the Indian state of Kerala, where food stamps and fair-price shops have helped to reduce child deaths to a half or even a third of the rate now prevailing in most countries at the same level of economic development. And it is because of the demonstrated benefits which such subsidies can bring to the life and health of the poorest of the world's children that the idea of an internationally backed food subsidy programme for the poorest of the poor — designed specially to reach undernourished pregnant women and young children — deserves urgent study.

In practice, effectively targeted food subsidies would also depend on social organisation*. If community development workers were to be involved in such schemes, for example, then there would be obvious advantages in cost-effectiveness. It would enable the subsidised food to be targeted far more flexibly and precisely to those at risk — to the poorest, to the pregnant woman, to the breastfeeding mother, to the young child, to those who have lost weight through repeated illness, to those whose growth chart indicates need. Potentially, it would also mean that the subsidised food could be made available in poorer villages or neighbourhoods rather than in whole regions or cities. Similarly, it might be made available at particular seasons rather than all the year round. In the rainy and usually hungry months before the harvest, for example, a food subsidy might mean that the

---

*The UNICEF-sponsored Integrated Child Development Services in India are one example of such a flexible community-based basic services approach. 'Anganwadis' (pre-school 'courtyard centres') have been established in poor communities. In each, a local woman with four month's training in community development is working with the people to provide supplementary food, immunisation, health and nutrition education, and primary health care. The All India Institute of Medical Sciences has found that the proportion of children with severe malnutrition has been reduced by half in the first thirty-three ICDS blocks surveyed. Each block contains approximately 100,000 people. The programme is currently being expanded to 600 communities in India.

poor would not have to take 'consumption loans' from money-lenders or landlords. And as one small example of how short-term help for those in need can dovetail with the needs of long-term development, not having to take out a loan may mean not having to sell land. And for the smallholder, it usually takes only two or three such loans to become landless.

In its briefing to Ministers of Agriculture in March of 1982, the Secretariat of the World Food Council (WFC) reported that 'if the trend of growing numbers of hungry people is to be reversed in this decade and mass hunger overcome, more direct measures will be required. . . It is now understood that general economic growth and increased agricultural production will not in themselves achieve a reduction in the absolute numbers of the hungry — an objective to which the international community is committed in principle.'

The 'direct measures' in the WFC recommendations included investment in credit, training and technology for small cultivators to enable them to produce more food for themselves and their families; redirecting food-aid towards the hungry (two-thirds of all food-aid today is sold on the open market where the poor must compete with the not-so-poor); and consumer food-subsidies targeted to those most in need.

Overall, the World Food Council now estimates that four billion dollars a year for the next fifteen years could provide the 'income and productive assets sufficient for about 500 million people to satisfy their minimum food needs by the end of the century.' Approximately two-thirds of that money would be for investment in small cultivators to generate both more food production and more incomes.

Added to the estimated cost of universal child immunization, and the promotion of the means and the knowledge for oral rehydration therapy, child growth charts, the breastfeeding of infants, and basic community services for primary education and health care, the total additional cost of such 'direct measures' to overcome the worst aspects of large-scale hunger and malnutrition would be in the region of six billion dollars a year until the end of the 1990s. In other words, one hundredth of the world's spending on armaments each year could go a long way towards increasing the health, nutrition and productivity of the poorest members of the human family and repairing the broken rungs which have left them stranded at the bottom of development's ladder.

Symptom and cause

In summary, immediate and dramatic gains against child malnutrition and ill-health are now offered by the availability of oral rehydration therapy, the immunis-ation of all children, the promotion of breast-feeding, and the mass use of child growth charts*. These four oppor-tunities to revolutionise child health are the leading edge of the continuing drive, by communities and parapro-fessional development workers, to work towards basic services for all — including health and nutrition educa-tion, basic literacy, cleaner water, and safer sanitation. In such a context, making available the means of spacing births is both more possible to do and more likely to find acceptance. And at that point, family planning itself could

---

*For the purposes of recalling the main elements of the child health revolution which is now possible, some in UNICEF now use the mnemonic GOBI-FF to stand for Growth charts, Oral rehydration therapy, Breastfeeding, and Immunization — plus the more difficult but equally vital elements of Food supplements and Family planning. Of course in any country, the key elements may differ.

also make a major contribution towards improving the health of mothers and children.

Secondly, and in addition to these methods of helping mothers and children to make the best use of the food they have available, some kind of targeted food subsidy — especially in pregnancy and infancy —will be indispensable if the grip of malnutrition on the 100 million children of the very poorest families is to be broken.

Third, the pressure needs to be kept up on the longer-term and more fundamental solution of increasing the productivity of the poor through greater social justice — including, above all, access to land and the means to make it grow more.

This wedge of different activities — operating on different time scales and against different degrees of financial constraint and political resistance — could break into the cycle of hunger which has trapped so many for so long.

Many of those fundamental changes which are necessary to expunge the stain of malnutrition and life-denying poverty from the fabric of our civilisation will be slow and painful. Land reform and employment creation on a scale commensurate with the scale of the problem will not happen over-night.

In the meantime, UNICEF itself is committed to that part of this same task which would most directly help individual mothers and children to improve their levels of health and nutrition *now*. And we believe that the very specific proposals outlined in this report could bring about such improvements in a short time and on a significant scale.

But we also believe that the now-possible 'children's revolution' in nutrition and health is in itself a part of the longer-term solution to hunger and poverty. For as the

Director General of the World Health Organisation has said, 'malnutrition is both one of the consequences of social injustice and one of the factors in its maintenance.'

In recent years, the mechanism of that maintenance has also become more clearly understood. In a child, the first reaction to inadequate food — to inadequate energy intake — is the reduction of energy output by the cutting down of 'discretionary activity'. But as is now widely known, 'discretionary activity' — including play — is essential to a child's development. As one new study puts it: 'the apathy and reduced physical activity of the malnourished child diminishes his interaction with the environment and deprives him of stimulating experiences and learning opportunities which may never come again.' More specifically, a now well-known study has shown how even at the age of three, undernourished children can already be one year behind their well-nourished contemporaries in language development.

And just as a child copes with malnutrition at the expense of personal development, so a malnourished adult copes at the expense of economic and community development. A relatively small reduction in food, for example, can have a significant effect on an adult's 'discretionary activity'. Similarly, specific dietary deficiency can also reduce energy. In one World Bank study in Indonesia, agricultural workers suffering from the 'invisible malnutrition' of anaemia were found to be 20 per cent less productive than their non-anaemic co-workers.

If levels of food intake are not sufficient for 'discretionary activity' then the effects of 'moderate' malnutrition are felt in the community as well as in the field or factory. Attending adult literacy classes, fencing a new vegetable garden, or participating in a village water supply scheme — investments of energy in the development of family and community life — all fall firmly into the category of 'discretionary activity' which is the first victim of 'moderate' malnutrition.

Less frequently researched, but even more important, is the female half of this same story. Usually consuming less than the 'bread-winner' whilst at the same time working much longer hours and coping with the additional energy demands of frequent pregnancy and breastfeeding, the woman lives even closer to the margins of serious malnutrition. According to the World Bank's 1980 World Development Report, for example, 'a variety of evidence indicates that in most developing countries women receive a lower proportion of their food requirements than adult men'.

Many women therefore have no other choice but to also cut down on 'discretionary activities', activities which might include carrying a one-year-old child to the nearest clinic to be weighed or vaccinated, participating in a new poultry farming or vegetable growing scheme at the other end of the village, or walking more miles for firewood so that water can be boiled before mixing it with an infant's weaning food. Not surprisingly, participation in improvements such as health clinics fall away markedly as the distance between home and health centre increases. And 'moderate malnutrition' therefore has a double impact on the child, striking once in the direct physiological consequences on the child's personal development, and again in its similarly restraining effect on the development of the society in whose care that child grows. For in the last analysis, development itself is a 'discretionary activity'.

That is why the direct attack on child malnutrition as a symptom of poverty is also an important part of the attack on the cause of that poverty. And the child health revolution which UNICEF believes is now possible would not only bring direct and immediate benefits to the children of today but also enable them to participate more fully in, and benefit more fully from, the wider social and economic changes which are necessary to abolish the poverty from which that hunger grows.

With the commitment to that revolution which its potential deserves, it is clear that the most effective attack ever made on child malnutrition could now be mounted — and that progress for children could again accelerate.

Without that commitment, the present slow-down of progress will continue and the target of halving the infant and child death rate in the year 2000 — with all that such an achievement would imply for the nutrition and health of the world's children — will be quietly abandoned.

If such a target, accepted by the international community only two years ago, is indeed laid by, then it means that the number of children who die unnecessarily each year from now on will be the equivalent of the entire under-five population of the United States of America or of the combined child populations of the United Kingdom, France, West Germany, Italy and Spain. Yet their voice is not heard in this debate and no murmur of protest do they make.

In a world distracted by so many deceptive and dangerous kinds of progress, we refuse to accept that such truly human and truly civilised progress as saving the lives and improving the health of the world's children should be abandoned at the first sign of difficulty. And we believe that if the political will can be found to seize the opportunities now offered by recent social and scientific progress, then the goal of adequate food and health for the vast majority of the world's children need not be a dream deferred.

PART II
IDEAS IN ACTION

The Rains

A report from a village in Yatenga, Upper Volta

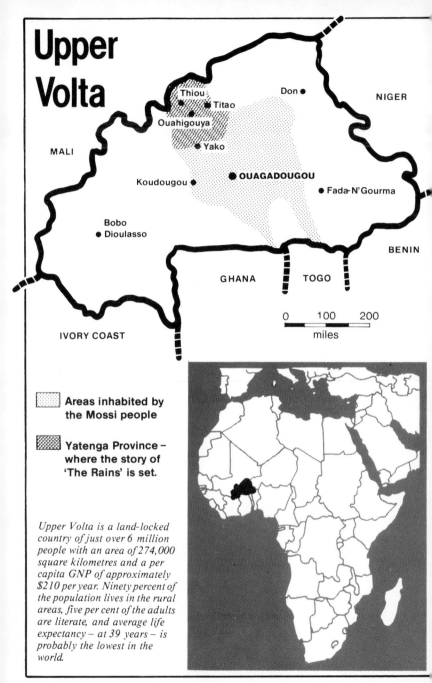

Upper Volta

Thiou

Titao

Ouahigouya

Yako

Don ●

OUAGADOUGOU

Koudougou ●

● Fada-N'Gourma

Bobo
● Dioulasso

NIGER

MALI

BENIN

GHANA   TOGO

IVORY COAST

0   100   200
miles

Areas inhabited by
the Mossi people

Yatenga Province –
where the story of
'The Rains' is set.

*Upper Volta is a land-locked
country of just over 6 million
people with an area of 274,000
square kilometres and a per
capita GNP of approximately
$210 per year. Ninety per cent of
the population lives in the rural
areas, five per cent of the adults
are literate, and average life
expectancy – at 39 years – is
probably the lowest in the
world.*

46

List of Illustrations

Photographs by Peter Williams (except for pages 51 and 57)

51

Acknowledgements:

*The characters of Assita and Hamade and the village of
'Samitaba', as well as all the incident and content of the
following account, are drawn from research and interviews with
actual villagers in the province of Yatenga during the early rains
of 1982.*

*That research would not have been possible without the
knowledge, perception and commitment of Marie Toure-
N'Gom and Anne-Marie Gaudras of UNICEF Abidjan, and
Bernadette Kabré of the Ministry of Education, Ouagadougou,
Upper Volta. The quality of their assistance and research was
directly related to their empathy with the people of Yatenga and
it was a privilege to work with them.*

*I would also like to thank Ahmed Mostefaoui, Regional
Director for UNICEF West Africa, and Stanislas Adotevi,
UNICEF Resident Programme Officer in Upper Volta — and
their staffs — for their cooperation and help. Similarly, thanks
are due to the staff and members of 'Six S' and the Naam
movement in Yatenga. In particular, Bernard Ledea
Ouedraogo, founder of the modern Naam movement, and
Ramata Sawadogo, Naam health and education officer, were
generous with their time and their patience. Whilst stressing that
this report is the responsibility of the writer alone, my thanks also
to Margaret Murray-Lee and all those who helped her to so
thoroughly check the accuracy of this account, and particularly
of its descriptions of Mossi culture and custom.*

*Finally, I would like to express my admiration and thanks to
the villagers of Yatenga themselves who welcomed me into their
homes and gave me their time and their help.*

Peter Adamson 1.12.82

*A thirty-minute documentary based on 'The Rains' will be made
by BBC Television during 1983. Versions of the film may also
be available in different languages during the year. For details
of availability, please write to Bernard Gerin, Chief of Radio
Film and Television Services, UNICEF, 866 UN Plaza,
New York NY 10017.*

The Rains

THE SKY has been overcast all day, heavy with the promise of rain. And with the evening come the first warm drops, spilt from the over-brimming air onto the dust of the compound.

Under thatched eaves, a woman crouches in the doorway, watching the patterning earth. Dark blots appear on the terracotta jars stacked in the open by the dead fire. Across the small courtyard an old blackboard, long ingrained with chalk, is being spattered by drops of black rain. In a few minutes the earth's slow stain is complete but still Assita, second of the three wives of Hamade Ouedraogo, remains in the doorway.

Over the low earth wall which her own hands helped to shape many years ago, she sees the water running from the thatched roof of her husband's hut. The clouds have brought the evening early and already the loose door of woven rushes has been pulled into place across the entrance. Just beyond are the huts of the other wives. On one the thatch is grey and brittle, darkened by the rain. On the other water runs easily off the still supple straw, raw edged and palely yellow in the last of the day's light.

The rain, hesitant at first, is now beginning to insist. On the flat-roofed building, the only one in the compound, water is pouring from a clay pipe high on the wall. In the morning, when the first rains have washed the roof, a jar will be placed over the muddy depression where tonight loose water splatters heavily onto the earth. Somewhere nearby an infant cries a cry of hunger and is suddenly silenced at the breast.

Now the guttering pipe and the hard rhythm of the rain are the only sounds to be heard in the compound. And over the vanishing outline of the village, the first soft far-off lightning plays around the edges of the sky. Looking out as she reaches for the rush door, Assita wonders whether it is also raining in her own village and, for a moment, she imagines her own mother lying awake, listening to the same sounds under the same sky.

Inside in the darkness she slowly undresses. On the rumpled cloths her two year old son has been asleep since long before the rains began. Behind him, lying on their sides against the curved wall, her twin daughters are also now asleep. As she steps over their folded dresses, the thought crosses her mind that, from tomorrow, all their clothes will need much more washing.

Lying in the darkness listening to the deadened sound of the rain on the heavy thatch, Assita remembers how the rain sounded on the tin roof of the nutrition centre all those years ago, how impossible it had been to sleep under the loud drumming of its fingers. They had been the first rains in almost two years. And they had come too late.

At the end of the second dry August, the people had sat in the shade of the empty granaries or under the doorways and walls of the compound, almost everything around them turned to the same parched colour so that only the harsh light and dusty shade defined the familiar shapes of the village. The women still walked to buy cans of water when they could and the men came and went looking for work. But the elders scarcely moved from morning to night and no children played.

'Yel Ka-ye,' people said when you asked how they

were — 'no problems'. 'Yel Ka-be', they smiled — 'no complaints'. 'Laafi Bala', murmured the elders – 'I have peace and health'. And they were all starving. Every live leaf had been collected and even in the towns it was said there was no food. Finally, when even the red millet had gone and roots were being boiled, the time came when the infants began to be given back.

For Lassana, her first child, tonight would have been the twelfth rains. Tomorrow he would have been working in the fields by her side, his supple arms wielding his own 'daba' blade into the wet earth. His action would not have been as economical as her own, but she knew he would have refused to straighten his back before his mother paused. And then the sweat would have run down his tapered body between shining shoulders, and those with daughters to marry would have taken notice. At midday, he would have sat and talked with her in the shade of the neem tree, hands clasped round strong legs caked with dried splashes of the red earth. Nearby, his father would have watched and said nothing. But as the season wore on, the elders would have nodded their heads as her son passed by.

Then, in the darkness, her son came to her as he was in the last days. And she saw again the loose folds of the empty buttocks and the clustered sores on the perished skin; saw the veinless swellings on the tops of both his feet and the helpless wooden charm around his wrinkled neck; saw again the taut skin of the old man's head on the infant's body and the agitated look in his lovely eyes.

Then she saw Hamade. It was the first time she had ever seen her husband carrying the baby close to him, like a woman. And her mind had clung to how unusual it was to see a man carrying a child like that and she had almost laughed, suspending its meaning in the air, refusing to allow its truth to touch the ground. Dully, as Hamade walked away, she recognised the custom that only a man shall carry an infant to the grave, and it sank into her soul that Lassana was cold against his chest.

Outside in the darkness of the small courtyard, water is running in a thousand rivers down the rough terrain of the mud wall, picking out pieces of gravel, exposing the ends of straws. On the ground the shallow thirst of the compact earth is already slaked and reddening pools are swirling over its surface.

Surging under the raised granaries, floating away chaff and straw and dragging along loose stones, the waters pour into a channel and turn for the gap in the compound wall. Under the open night, water from all directions is swirling down each imagined incline, flooding each imperceptible hollow, pouring into troubled pools and overflowing into broad white-flecked streams across the countryside. By the encircled wall, an old and leaky water-bucket, made from the inner-tube of a tyre, is moving along the level ground.

Overhead the storm bends over the village like a Mossi dancer, body poised motionless over limbs which hammer on the earth so fast it seems that nothing could increase their beat until teeth are bared and eyes stare and in a final frenzy of the drums, the feet blur like humming birds' wings in an unsustainable ecstasy of dance.

In the porous laterite under the soil, the rain is being sucked through a thousand crannies, seething through every crack and fissure, rushing along the centuries of smoothed galleries, pouring into streams and surging over waterfalls to deposit itself into the dark safes of water under the Sahel.

But tonight not even the hydroptic earth can drink enough and across its surface the rejected waters turn away bad-temperedly, a restless reddening tide scouring the earth for another way of escape.

In its way, a small and leafless shrub, unrecognisable as a young neem tree, finds itself marooned by unaccustomed water. For eight months it has survived the white sun and the browsing goats. Now, rupturing the water's flow, the plant bends its stem to accommodate the angry ripple at its base. Unappeased, the tide streams by on either side, seducing away the soil from around the slender shoot. Slowly, lasciviously, the waters reveal the tender whiteness of the young tree's root. Then, in an instant, the tree is gone, persuaded out of the ground, lifted as painlessly as a child's first tooth. A second later, a little binding of red earth, freed from the grip of the roots, follows after it like a small clot in the haemorrhaging blood of the soil, swept away to find the sudden streams and rivers which tonight are carrying the soil of Upper Volta south to the Ivory Coast, Ghana, and the cold waters of the Atlantic.

IN THE MORNING the earth is red and raw under a cloudless sky. Across its stillness a donkey brays, dislodging the first hooded crows from their nests, rustling the chickens in the loose straw, breaking the sleep of the village.

Soon the first fires are being kindled between stone hobs and across the compounds come the familiar sounds of the

63

morning, of water being splashed into iron pots, firewood being pulled out into the open, the first grains being ground under rough stones, calabashes being scoured out with handfulls of harsh straw, children solemnly pounding green leaves in wooden mortars, baobob or the sour wild sorrel, ready to be boiled into sauces for the morning meal.

Between huts and granaries, in the beaten earth paths and passageways, groups of men are discussing the night's rains, some holding a warm drink, made with tamarind water to soften the new chill in the dawn. In the low-walled open kitchens, the women of Samitaba are moving about bent double at the waist, not bothering to straighten their backs between the morning tasks: pushing dry twigs a little further under the fire, stirring the sauce with a peeled stick, sieving the steamed neere seeds through handfulls of fine straw, adding the ground millet flour, little by little, to the boiling water.

Close to the opening in the compound wall, Assita is crouching by her hearth. With a curved fragment of a broken clay jar she scrapes the last of the porridge from the steaming pot into a large calabash on the ground. In a smaller black pan, wedged by a stone between the larger stones of the fireplace, the dark brown sauce bubbles thickly. The elders and the men have already been served and now Hamade's five younger children are sitting on the damp floor around the steaming bowl, left hands gripping its rim as they eat the smooth porridge, tinged faintly pink by the few unwinnowed flecks of the dark-red husk. Assita joins them, dipping puckered fingers into the hot brown sumbala and making sure that her just-weaned son has his share.

Soon she is on her feet again, back bent, splashing a little water into the scraped-out cooking pots. With a last word to her daughters, she takes up the tin of water which had been put to warm on the last of the breakfast fire and turns to leave the crowded kitchen.

In the privacy of the small walled area behind her own hut, she pours the warm water over her face and body, working into a thin lather the crumbly white soap, made in the dry season. Feeling faintly sick as she rinses her face with the last of the warm water, she reaches out a hand to the mud wall to steady herself and looks down at the lid of the clay jar standing in the corner of the washroom. It is almost three months now since she has had to use the folded strips of clean cotton in the jar.

Hurrying a little now, she wraps on her oldest fupoko and steps out of the washroom. The other wives will soon be waiting at the wall.

Across the landscape groups of figures are already bent over their fields. Most of the village has been out since soon after dawn, for these are the valuable hours when the earth is still soft and the air is still cool. The rains will last only four months at the most; four months in which the land must be made to grow enough for the year.

Already the night's streams have disappeared and even the rivers will by now be beds of mud in which cattle are leaving deep oozy hoof-prints as they graze the pools. Only the Black Volta, more than a hundred kilometres away, flows all the year round. But here in Yatenga, the soil which yesterday would have answered the hoe only with a cloud of dust, can today be dug into, turned, planted. And as the morning sun climbs over the Sahel, a million dabas rise and fall.

One of them is gripped by the hardened hands of Assita Ouedraogo, working together with her two co-wives, scraping hollows at regular intervals in the wet earth ready for the planting of grain. Within calling distance her husband, Hamade, works alone on a shoal of land between two footpaths, hoeing furrows of the broken heavy earth across the line of a scarcely perceptible slope.

Coming to the end of a row, Hamade straightens his back and stands for a moment, his sleeveless cotton shift, the colour of the earth, standing off his shoulders and making him look even broader than he is. As he rests, he contemplates what his neighbours are doing, which fields they have decided to work first, whose sons are working with them and whose are not. No hedged rectangles, no fences or ditches, tell him where one neighbour's land ends and another's begins. It is something he learnt while working these fields at his father's side, as now he works them with his own sons, gradually coming to know the shapes and peculiarities of the village fields in the same way as he came to recognise the faces and characters of village people. One field starts where the earth dips beyond the footpath and ends at the wide area of thin clay, like an unbroken skin on the surface of the earth, which is the field of the ancestors. Another field begins by the termite hill and ends at that invisible and meandering line between soil and shale, earth and sand, a dividing line of judgement between fertility and barrenness, marked by a fence of decisions that, beyond it, labour will be in vain. And as his educated eye recognises the contours and boundaries of the land, so it also sees its virtues and vices: a depression in the earth probably means that soil has lodged there and that maize will do well; a darker patch has held its moisture well and can probably take sorghum again; a subtle change of colour means that the soil is too sandy and that millet had better be sown. Memory and the look and feel of the earth under the hoe tell him when a field should rest for another year, though even this morning Hamade has had to decide that fields which a farmer would leave fallow, a father must plant with food.

Normally, the first day of the rains and the beginning of work brings with it a release of tension. For eight long months the level of the grain in the mud-built granaries has been steadily falling without anyone being able to do anything about it . . . until it rains. Now, at last, the work of restocking the granaries tight to their thatched roofs can at least begin. But for Hamade this morning, anxiety is not lessened as he swings the smooth handled daba, feet slightly apart in the wet plastic sandals, and watches the soil breaking under the blows from his body.

An hour ago, as he reached into the sweet-smelling dimness of the granary to pull out the day's ration of grain, he had seen the granary floor. There are four more months to go to the harvest. Once again he has failed to make 'the sesuka', 'the welding', the joining of the last harvest to the next.

His family will not starve. Somehow the grain will be bought. It will be bought with the money buried in a tin under the floor of his hut, saved from the last time he left his home for the dry season and travelled a thousand miles by train to work for wages on the coffee plantations of the Ivory Coast. Or it will be bought by selling a few goats and sheep, or by borrowing money from his relations, or by going to the Naam warehouse in the town. The grain will be found. But he had hoped that the granaries would last a little longer, that he would only have to buy grain for two months, not four.

Instead, he has had to decide that he will, after all, take up his friend's offer of a lift into town for the meeting this afternoon. At the same time, he will be able to bring back a sack of grain on the cart.

Hamade's forehead is glistening like the earth now as he

67

strikes into the heavy soil and begins to break another ridge across the land. However unjustified the feeling may be, Hamade still feels the shame of having to go into town for grain. It is a feeling embedded in the centuries, rooted in the culture of necessity, a part of his sense of himself. Salt and spices can be bought with money, even neere or karite can be bought with money. But staple grains you grow with your own hands. And you grow enough to stretch across the seasons and make 'the sesuka', the joining. If you are known to be buying grain in the months before the harvest, or if you are seen to be seeking to exchange red millet for white*, then it is a matter of shame. You are lazy, you have not worked, or you are not prudent, you are not a good manager. And you are not worthy of your family.

Circumstances have changed. And Hamade knows that there is not a man in Samitaba this morning who has enough grain to last until October. At the very least, shame should be diluted by the numbers of the shamed. But whatever the reason and no matter how many others are in the same position, Hamade is still disturbed, still feels the dishonour of seeing the granary floor on a morning in June. Not to be able to grow enough grain affects the way he feels as he works the land, subtly changes his sense of himself as he walks through the village and exchanges greetings with the elders, or sits down in his compound to eat with his wives and his children.

Reaching the end of another row he straightens again and looks over his shoulder, roughly comparing what has been done with what is still to do. And as he looks around

*The inferior red millet is used mainly for making 'dolo' the local millet beer. The more respectable white millet is used for flour.

the family's lands, screwing up his eyes against the climbing sun, the feeling inside hardens into something close to anger as he sees again the evident truth that, to fill only two granaries, he and his family are working harder and more prudently than his ancestors ever did to fill three.

Up by the village wall, on the 'beoogla', the vegetable plots of his wives, he can see Assita's two daughters dragging out firewood to be stored on the soil. As it dries ready for the kitchen fire, the stock of wood will help to break the flow of the rains and hold the moisture in the soil while the branches entangle the wind, frustrating its attempt to blow away the surface of the soil, and its leaves slowly rot to enrich the earth as they shade the damp land and young seedlings from the sun.

In the millet fields across the path, he knows that his wives are planting one black-eyed niebe bean for every three grains of millet in each scraped hollow of earth. Around the feebler grain, the bean roots will help to bind the soil and keep the moisture as they grow. Through the long dry months, he knows that the seeds themselves have been cared for, buried in earthenware jars full of fine ash from the fires. In the weeks to come, if the rains continue to fall, then the land will be hoed once more, tired dabas scraping small fortresses of earth around each fresh green shoot to defend them against invading rain or tugging wind.

Hamade bends his back to the earth again, breaking off another ridge of soil. And now the nagging blade of his daba is nearing the first of the two lines of shin-high purple stones, arranged like a broad arrow pointing up the slight slope. Last night, as the rains coursed over the land, this heavy stone prow forced the waters away down either side of this, his most fertile field. Many times during the long hot dry season he had wondered if the stones were worth it as he and his sons had brought them one-by-one — all one hundred and twelve of them — on the back of his aging bicycle from the low hills four kilometres away. But this morning, the smooth shallow channel on the far side of the line of stones tells him that their efforts were not in vain. No soil was carried away by the night's rains. And now, behind the stone prow's protection, the droppings of sheep, goats and donkey are sparsely spread, waiting to be dug in along with the winnowings of the pounded grain, the peanut shells, and the scattered ash. As the daba moves on, the first of his sons comes dragging an old cardboard box, soggy after the night's rains, and lays it to rot in the middle of the maize field.

———————

By midday, the landscape is almost deserted as all living things walk, fly or crawl from under the vertical sun. In the village, the elders sleep lightly in their open doorways, chickens brood under the granaries, and even the marauding goats are penned up in the narrow strip of shade under the village walls. In the fields the 'wife of the rain', the brilliant magenta beetle which appears on the surface only after it has rained – and is loved for it – has disappeared down dark passageways.

Under the neem tree, Hamade rests, the field more than half done. It is Ramadan, and he will not eat until the sun goes down. Looking out across the landscape, cleansed of the tiring dust, the sun glistening on the shale, the beauty of its colours after the night's rains forces itself into his drowsy gaze. But to his eyes it is a tragic beauty. For he knows, as all who work the earth of Yatenga know, that it should not look like this. Within the memory of his father, these fields were rich openings of brown soil cut or burnt

70

into the forest and savannah. Underneath lay the laterite, the iron-bearing rock and shale whose naked outcrops could only be seen on the broken sides of the hills. Now it is this scarce-hidden rock and shale, so much of its topsoil gone, which gives the morning's landscape its brittle red beauty.

Hamade cuts idly at a clod of earth with his resting daba. Already, a thin crust of dried soil has formed on its surface. Sand, gravel, shale, soil, it is this earth which yields a little less food at each harvest, this earth which now fills two granaries instead of three, this earth which leaves the ends of 'the sesuka' a little further apart each year. The earth, and the rains. If the rains would fall as they used to, and if they would stay in the soil instead of running off and taking its richness with them, little by little, then the earth would again grow enough to stretch across the seasons.

Hamade closes his eyes, at first in rest against the strong light, and soon in almost conscious sleep as his back relaxes against the tree.

Down either side of his face run the three curved lines of scars, cut there earlier than he can remember. In the past, these lines would have been his protection. No Mossi would fight another. No Mossi would sell another into slavery. And safety resided in recognition. That is why the Mossi identity is so proudly inscribed upon this face. Ouedraogo — 'the horseman' — the name that goes back almost a thousand years to the legendary warrior, born of a Ghanaian princess, who founded the first Kingdom of the Mossi. Hamade — 'the eyelids' — the name of the invading Fulani who, a hundred years ago, killed a Mossi Chieftan and whose feared trademark was his perpetually swollen eyelids.

Much has happened to the people of the three Mossi

kingdoms of Upper Volta during those hundred years. It has been a century of erosion, a century which has scoured at the sense of self-worth of a people, washed over pride in culture and faith in tradition, eroded the soil of confidence from around the roots of capacity.

First had come the erosive wave of colonialism, confronting the Mossi with military superiority and judging their culture to be backward in science and technology, primitive in religion and economics, barbaric in manners and customs. And with colonialism had come the beginning of the retreat into the dark caves of self-doubt.

Soon came the decades of forced labour on the plantations and on the thousand-mile railroad to the coast, sluicing the strength of the men from the villages and harnessing it to the exploiting of their own land. And when the forced labour had stopped, economic migrations had taken its place. More than a third of all the men had left their villages to look for wages, eroding the community both by their departure and by their return, bringing with them new ways and values, new music and new stories. And with them had come the new radios, wrist watches, and motor bikes – not a single component of which could be made in a Mossi village.

Finally, there had come the years without rain. More than a memory, a part of the very matrix by which other memories and perceptions are assimilated, the drought seared the existence of the Sahel. In the trees and plants and grasses it has withered, in the land it has left naked and brittle, the 'wárè' seemed to reach out across time as well as across the space of Africa, blighting the invisible future with its touch. Now, when the rains fall, they do not stay on the land and the soil enriches the water as much as the water the soil. And when the Harmattan winds blow in

February and March, soil as loose as chaff at the winnowing flies with them to the west.

In Yatenga this morning, the drought of ten years ago can still be felt. For it was a time which gnawed at the very capacity of the land to regenerate itself, just as the decades of erosion of culture and confidence have threatened the powers of recovery of the Mossi.

Hamade Ouedraogo opens his eyes. In the midday heat the tired pallor of the land is returning, its freshness fading as its surface yields up its moisture to the irresistable sun. His eyes travel across to the village, its walls the colour of the soil, its huts and granaries the differently lit facets of that same earth, its thatched roofs graded in shape and colour by the years. In all his gaze, the only alien colour is the blue plastic sheet made from a torn fertiliser bag and stretched instead of thatch over the four poles of a shelter in the fields below.

Hamade stands. In the wrinkles of his knees and ankles, the mud has dried to fine lines of clay. In the maize field his two eldest boys, the sons of his first wife, are already bending their backs to the work.

Stepping back over the line of stones, he glances at the areas he has allotted to the boys. The patch from the termite hill to the end of the line of stones is quite a lot for his eldest boy to tire his muscles on in an afternoon. But not, as he has often thought, for a man to feed his family on for a lifetime.

Setting to with a will, Hamade's daba cuts into the already raw and wounded earth, its blade red and wet as it picks and scrapes at his family land. For some reason his mood has changed, optimism and determination replacing the remembered bitterness of the morning. It is one of those swings of mood which is difficult to ascribe to any particular circumstance, though it may be that working with his sons alongside adds something more than muscle to the task.

Soon the steady economical rhythm of the daba frees his mind for other things, wandering ahead to the Naam meeting under the trees which he and his neighbour will attend this afternoon, and to the grain he must bring back. There will be some grumbling at the meeting and the attendance today might be poor. No-one likes to lose time away from the fields when the rain has just fallen and some of the Naam leaders will have had to leave their villages before noon. But tension has been slowly growing between local ORD* officials and the Naam groups and the meeting has been called to clear the air. Hamade's presence is not essential. He is only the secretary of the Samitaba Naam group and he probably would not be going were it not for the chance to bring the hundred kilo sack of grain back on the cart.

As they progress towards the narrower end of the field, father and sons gradually converge until they are working almost side-by-side on the land. Before long, the three dabas are rising and falling in a common rhythm, a rhythm which no-one wants to break. Hamade smiles to himself. This is the way to finish a field, the way of the Naam. Slowing down the pace a fraction, conscious for a few more years of his own greater stamina, he remembers the traditional Naams of his own youth.

As a way of working, Naam means many things in the Moore language. But to those who have grown up in the Mossi culture, its meaning needs no explanation. All of the adults, all of the elders, took part in the traditional Naams, working together in unison to hoe the fields of the

*The Organisation Regionale pour le Developpement is the government body responsible for rural development activities in the eleven regions of Upper Volta.

74

chief, or of the elderly, or of the sick. And its unique place in Mossi tradition is one reason why the fight back of the Mossi of Yatenga against what is happening to their lands and their lives is based on the idea of the Naam. For it is a fight back which is as much to do with arresting the erosion of pride in the culture and capacity of a people as it has to do with arresting the erosion of the land itself.

Hamade is the first to straighten his back. His sons give one or two more blows to the earth and then casually straighten too, faces not showing the pain in bicep and wrist. After a few seconds, they look back on the land they have turned over. One more session like the last and the field will be done. And as they stand near the end of the patch of land, breathing becoming shallower as the pain mellows to an ache, Hamade remembers the excitement of the Naam, of holding up one of a long line of dabas poised in the air, awaiting the drums. On either side, shoulder to shoulder, the line stretched out across the field, the atmosphere of a festival in the air, boys in their loose blue 'Kuryogyogo' and girls arranged in groups of friends who had sewn matching tops and headscarves from the same printed cottons. After an age, a hush would fall on the field from nowhere. All eyes catch the movement of the Naaba Bãoogo's arm as he signals to release the raised hands of the drummers and to the boom of the gãgãado and the calabash bendre and the rattle of the lunga, a hundred dabas fall into the field.

And now the shuffling legs of the village youth are hidden by dust and some dabas rise as others fall, struggling for the beat. Suddenly, they are all swinging into the earth together in an unbreakable rhythm and confident feet are moving off down the field in time to the music. In front, the troubadours step backwards before the advancing line of dabas, the buffalo horn flute flowing behind to link the staccato of the tam-tams. Pursuing them, the dabas rise and fall, preceded by a bow wave of dust and trailing behind a wake of freshly turned soil, as if a plough with a hundred blades, the full width of the field, were being dragged through the earth by the irresistable tractor of the drums.

Just as suddenly, the noise would stop and a few straggling dabas would bite audibly into the earth. Then backs would straighten as the dust slowly died and heads would turn to see how far they had come. They would be excited and a little embarrassed, exchanging smiles as talk broke out and the skin of the girls shone in the sunlight. Down the line, the Weem Naaba walks, the protector of the virgins, solicitous lest a note or a message should be smuggled to any of his charges during the Naam. Soon the line of flashing blades would move off again down the field under the influence of the drums. 'Stay in step!' the Toogo Naaba shouts, 'Watch your neighbour, dabas higher, dabas higher!' Along the sides of the field, the elders also raise their voices, 'Wa t'd maane', they shout, 'Come on let's work, be proud when you dig'. It had been different Hamade remembered, in the time of his father. Then they had shouted a new slogan down the line: 'Koy neere yaa nasaara tuumde', 'Cultivate well, it is for the white man'.

In two hours, a field that would have taken weeks of lonely dispiriting hoeing, a field that would have been too much for limbs grown old or frail, was freshly ploughed by the 'kombi-Naam', the Naam of the youth. There were many such Naams for different groups and different tasks, many traditional ways — like the Sosoga and the Sõng Taaba — of organising the community's resources, muscles, experience, crafts, music, into a unity of effort and a

---

*In the Moore language, 'to work' implies 'to eat'.

pride in achievement. And it is from the roots of this tradition that the new Naam movement has grown up in Yatenga.

With a grunt of encouragement, Hamade plants his feet again and brings the hoe up behind him. On the second stroke, his sons fall again into his rhythm, moving down the field towards the end of the day's work.

On the road by the village, a donkey and cart comes to a halt where the neere tree casts its broken shade over the red shale. While the boys take the dabas back to the compound, Hamade and his neighbour exchange greetings. In the fields Hamade's wives glance up, wondering why he is leaving the fields so early on a day when it has just rained. He has not told them why he is going into town anymore than he will tell them that the granaries are running low.

The journey into town will take about an hour, rolling slowly to the east as the men discuss the rains. Apparently the water collapsed one of the wells at Oufray during the night and carried away a part of the bulldozed earth-road to Yako.

The cart is leaving the village and now, on the left, a long linked-wire fence about the height of a man runs parallel to the road. Behind it, line after line of one-year-old trees, acacias, neems, zangas, stretch as far as the eye can see up the gently sloping hillside. As the cart passes the end of each straight row of saplings, Hamade looks down the line, enjoying again the symmetry of their work.

In the last rains, a new kind of Naam was organised in Samitaba. Working together, the villagers hoed two thousand hollows on this hillside and scraped mounds of soil over the planted seeds. The men had staked out the long perimeter fence, without which not a sapling would have survived the free grazing animals, and the women have since watered the young trees through the dry season, pulling a cart heavy with their collected water jars from the dam about a kilometre away.

On the corner of the fence hangs a black plank stencilled with the white letters 'NAAM — UNICEF'. The wire fencing, the first tree-seeds, and the cart for transporting the jars of water, came from outside. The labour came from the Naam group.

In perhaps five more years, the branches of this plantation will be the right thickness for kitchen fires and the trees will save the women that twelve hours a week of foraging further and further to fill the floppy wicker baskets with enough wood to cook the family's meals. They will also save the soil that even longer journey to the south by wind and water.

Hamade raises a hand to the elder sitting by the fence. The plantation is a small patch on the threadbare cloth of the Sahel. But a week ago, he was at the Naam committee meeting in the village where they had heard of other hectares being planted by the Naams of Somyaga, Titao and Oufray. In another two or three years, depending on the rains, the Samitaba trees themselves will have grown to a safe height and thickness. Then three sides of the wire fence will be uprooted and re-erected to surround another hectare of plantation. The committee had discussed moving faster. Someone has proposed that when the trees are high enough a small proportion of them should be cut down and used as new fence posts or sold to buy more seeds and wire. There had been those who were against cutting down any of the trees on principle. But Hamade had thought the suggestion made sense. Even a young tree sells for almost two dollars while a fence post is one dollar forty and a single seed is five cents. But it will be three years before the decision on the rate of expansion has to be made and the meeting had ended with the usual accounting for subscriptions, collected by the members of the committee and amounting to eight cents per week from each member of the village Naam. That money too will be put towards more wire.

The cart is almost at the end of the plantation now and the last serried ranks of trees march up the slope, a platoon where an army is needed. Then the fence also turns up the hillside and the cart rumbles on past the open hillside where five or six hardy bushes cling to an acre of red shale.

A SSITA and her co-wives are beginning the last line of the millet field, hoeing and scraping hollows at regular intervals. By now, rhythm and efficiency are compensating for tiredness as Assita and the youngest wife move together, perforating the earth for the first seeds. Behind them moves the eldest wife, a much-mended calabash held under her hand by a double string running across the back of her knuckles. Expertly, the finger and thumb roll the four seeds over the edge of the calabash, dropping them with bent back into the waiting hollow of the earth. Hardly pausing, the calabash moves on, while the first bare footstep shifts the earth back over the hole and the next presses gently down on the planted seeds.

Resting with both hands on top of the daba handle,

Assita surveys the stretch of disturbed earth which is the day's work. But from the earth there is no answering promise that the family of Ouedraogo will reap what they have sown today. For no employer is as fickle, kind or cruel, as the rains. If the night's downpour was a false start, if no more rains fall in the weeks to come, then the same sun which will make these plants push out fresh green shoots will turn and wither them in the ground until their pale brown fingers crumble to the touch. Then, if and when the rains begin anew, the wives of Hamade will return to plant this morning's field again. And each morning now will see anxious eyes cast to the skies. It is an anxiety which forms an invisible bond extending across the Sahel and even across seas to all those who wait and wonder whether the livelihood earned by labours past will see them through until the rewards of present labour fall due. For those in the cities working for money, it is the anxiety of Friday night's pay packet almost gone by Tuesday; for those in Samitaba who work for food, it is the anxiety of walking past the falling granaries and wondering whether the remainder of the last harvest will last until the next.

For the moment, the anxiety is eased by the beginning of the long process of replenishing the granaries. And for the shy youngest wife in particular, there is pleasure amounting almost to an excitement in the walk back to the village in the company of the two older women. On her marriage to Hamade seven months ago, she had felt his first two wives close ranks, sensed that her presence had forged a solidarity between them which had not been there before. They had not been unkind. But, imagined or real, she had felt a sense of exclusion which made worse the loneliness of leaving her own family and village for the first time, like the simultaneous closing of the door from which

80

you have come and the door to which you are going.

Today she had worked unobtrusively hard in the field, neither pausing to rest before the others nor continuing to work when they straightened their backs. Now, tired as they, she is part of what has been done, part of the replenishment of the granaries, part of the solidarity it has created. And, walking back, she is part of its conversation too. As the three women approach the village wall, her eyes feel hot with inexplicable tears. Just to be part of this casual intimate talk is all that she has wanted in the last few months. Perhaps it is now rather than at her marriage that a door is opening, her old life ending and her new one beginning. Perhaps this is to be the end of the long home-sickness of a fifteen year-old girl.

Inside the village, the women pass through the labyrinth of low earth walls to Hamade's compound. By its entrance stand the three granaries themselves, raised on dusty logs for the air to circulate, secure against rodents and sudden rains. High in the gravelly mud walls through which the ends of wooden beams protrude, a square door of planks, about the width of a man's shoulders, gives access to the dark womb. To reach the door, the smooth and barkless tree trunk lying on the passageway is propped up against the granary wall. Using the fork of the tree trunk as a step, it is just possible to reach the wooden latch of the door.

No woman has ever seen inside these granaries. Not even the first wife. Every morning after the early meal, Hamade steps up on the tree trunk and reaches down through the narrow opening into the sweet-smelling belly of the barn. Each morning he fills the same wicker basket, about the size of a baby's cradle, and hands it to whichever of his wives is on duty for the day. Then the door is latched closed and the tree trunk laid to the ground.

Years ago, in the time of another great drought, there

were women who saw that their husbands' barns were almost empty and who left to return to their own families and villages rather than face starvation in the 'sesuka'. That was in the reign of the Naaba Koabga, whose name means that he was chief in the year when the price of a sack of millet reached 500 cowrie shells. Such was the shame brought upon the men without enough food in their granaries to keep their wives that the old taboos were revived and the silent perfumed granaries were forbidden to the eyes of women.

Just outside the village wall stands the great grey mortar, the communal 'toore', hollowed from the trunk of a grainy tree more years ago than anyone can remember. Banished from the village itself because of the irritating white powder which flies from the stalks and grain at the first rough pounding, the mortar stands outside surrounded by a rough carpet of straw, husk, chaff and peanut shells, all the detritus of the pounding, among which the goats and chickens can always find something else to eat. And it is here that Assita brings that morning's wicker basket of sorghum which must last for three main meals.

Soon the heaviest pestle, smooth like the handles of the dabas, is rising and falling on the soft floury sorghum, thudding into the hard bowl of the mortar with the dull sound of the woman's drum, jolting the black-red beads of grain from the stalks and sending sudden sprays of powder into the air.

As the pestle passes up and down in front of her face, Assita sees through its movement to the goats browsing through the 'pagã puugo', the woman's field, close to the village walls. This year she will try to plant everything, chillies, onions, lettuce, okra, even groundnuts. But recently, every time Assita looks at the women's plots the same thought occurs: with the new water pump so close by, and with the cart for the plantation, the vegetable plot could be watered by hand. And crops could be grown in the dry season. It would be a foolish thing for one woman to attempt. A lonely patch of green would only feed the village goats. But if all the women were to water the pagã puugo, and if those with adjoining plots were to borrow the money for a fence and pay it back by selling vegetables... once more she makes up her mind that she will say something at the next meeting of the women's Naam.

After a day in the fields, the action of pounding with the 'tulugo' is too similar to hoeing with a daba not to be tiring to the arms and back. But after ten minutes the crushed and broken straw has been shaken from its grain. Holding a large calabash bowl high over her head, Assita tips its contents in a long graceful pour, watching the hard grains rattle accurately into the calabash at her feet, while the otherwise imperceptible movement of the air wafts straw and chaff gently to the waiting goats.

Hardly a grain is lost as Assita twice winnows the wicker basket-full and then puts the seeds alone back into the mortar. And now the pounding begins again, this time with a grittier thud as the pestle splits the hard backs of the dark red husks and releases the tiny white grains. But now, at the second pounding, an ache suffuses the arms of Assita as the heavy pestle flies and only rhythm can sustain the effort as the actions of her body merge into the numberless millions of blows struck by the 'tulugo' in the hands of Yatenga's women while her mind remains separate, hers alone, following its secret path over the contours of her circumstance. And as an old woman pauses on the path to the village, watching the pounding as she catches her breath in rest, Assita thinks of the time when she was watched in all her work, watched by the critical eyes of her husband's family.

83

Only by reputation had she known Hamade before their marriage. She knew he was in health and that he was considered a hard worker, prudent by nature, and respectful of the traditions. She knew he was thought to be kind and not one to work the earth by beating a wife if she did not hoe a set area of land before leaving the fields. Of this much her parents had satisfied themselves. And Assita had been relieved. For in this one decision almost all the possibilities of her life are circumscribed. And by the 'furbu', the benediction of marriage, the lines of happiness and well-being on the graph of her life are set on course as much as by the accident of birth itself.

Then had come her own inspection by the women of the Ouedraogo family who had watched her as she stood and walked, examined the shape of her breasts and legs; satisfied themselves that her feet were not turned outwards or her toes misshapen; watched to see that she was not ill-mannered and didn't look at other men; sent her for water to make sure that she did not look at the ground as she walked; even asked her to clap her hands in the air as she pounded the grain with the flying pestle. Anxiously her own mother had tried to make last minute corrections to her upbringing, checked her deportment, urged her to relax the neck and to stoop the head and body in submission, shouting at her not to hold her head back like a man.

But when she had carried water, when of necessity a woman is allowed to keep her back straight and her head high, she had known as all young women know that she was at her most attractive to a man. And she had seen Hamade looking at her, and known that her inspection would have a favourable result.

After the wedding, her husband's family had invited her to enter the hut of their ancestors. It was their final question. For no woman who was not a virgin would have dared to step inside its darkness. Rather, she would have confessed the name of her lover. Then the man would have been summoned. But after promising to stay away from each other forever, both would have been forgiven.

Assita had stepped inside the hut. Then after months made anxious by the fear of infertility had come her first pregnancy and the birth of Lassana.

'The water is spilt,' the elder women had told her when she had lost Lassana, 'but the jar is not broken.' Now she thinks of the announcement she must soon make to her husband's aunt, and of what will happen when the other women know that she is pregnant. One day soon she will be invited into the kitchen of the first wife and the other women of the compound will talk casually without any allusion to her pregnancy. Suddenly, without warning, one of them will bring an open hand from behind her back and slap the side of her face hard, knocking her across the small room and bringing tears to her eyes. 'You stole my salt', she will shriek, or 'You hit my child'. Now, anything that any of the women has ever suspected her of doing, every grudge that has been harboured, will be hurled at her, probably with more, lighter, blows.

As suddenly as it began the flow of abuse will stop and her husband's aunt, the first to be told of the pregnancy will come forward to congratulate her on the fulfilling of her duty. Then the other women will surprise and embarrass her with their memories of kind things she has done, things she didn't even think they had noticed. They will in turn parade her good qualities, presenting each one with an example from their own experience. By now very emotional, the praise will also bring tears and then the practical kindnesses will flow: the traditional massage from her husband's mother; meals made and brought to her by the other wives; gifts from other women in the village, and for her first child there had been protective beads for the hips or a text sewn up in a leather necklace. Best of all, there will be gifts of food from her own mother; not spices to make the unborn baby cry, not peanuts which will cause it to be born covered in too much greasy vernix, not eggs which may make the child into a thief, but fruit, milk, rice, nuts, oil and flour in calabashes and enamelled bowls.

Assita's thoughts return to the ache in her arms and the wooden mortar where white grains and dark husk now lie in roughly equal proportions. Finally the pounding can cease and the gentler winnowing begins again until the calabash bowl is almost level with white grains and the black cases of their heavier chaff. Crouching on her haunches, Assita begins to slap the orange calabash from hand to hand, jolting and rotating it at the same time, moving with the rhythm of yet another of the dances of her life, working the stubborn husks to the edges of the tilted bowl from which they are shaken, slap by slap, onto the waiting earth. Soon the bowl contains only the white grains, the heart of the matter, the end of the long process which began with the rain and the hoe. Carefully, Assita pours them into the metal measuring bowl. If a few too many stalks were put into the wicker basket from the granary this morning, then there will now be a little too much grain for the bowl. Today, Hamade's judgement was almost exact. Had there been any over, it would have been saved for the following day. There is no room for fluctuation. The family eats exactly the same amount of food each day. The amount of staples cannot be less or energy will fail. And it cannot be more — not even by one handful — because survival through the sesuka is not a matter of guesswork.

Inside her own compound, Assita leans against the kitchen wall for balance as she pulls on her sandals. In front of her stands the huge flat circle of the grinding area, waist high from the ground, into which are set the dozen narrow stones at regular intervals around the perimeter. Until three years ago, she would now have faced the hardest task of the day, standing at her own place on the circle, both hands gripping the top of the loose stone, rasping it forwards and scraping it back over the grains on the stone fixed in the circle, grinding the grain to the powder of flour. Even more than usual, she is glad of the mill today.

At the entrance to Hamade's mother's kitchen, she is told that her infant son is still sleeping. Already feeling the day's efforts in her back, she decides to leave him where he is. Her mother-in-law's calabashes of grain, covered like her own by tucked-in cloths, are picked up by her daughters. At eight years old, both can already carry a calabash on their heads with almost the same assurance as Assita herself.

Less than fifty paces from the village entrance, through which Assita and the two girls are now emerging, the youngest wife is working the arm of the pump with both hands. Today it is her turn to bring in the seven 14 litre jars which will meet the family's needs. Even more than the grinding, it was this which used to claim the most time and drain the most energy before the well was sunk. As the children go to exchange a few words with their aunt, they pass the small stencilled notice 'NAAM — UNICEF', put there when the pump was lowered into the well .

It is four years now since the men began to dig. At first the hole had been wide and progress swift as they went through earth and gravel. Then, as expected, the steel spike of the pick had begun to grate and clang against shale and then rock. It was a sound which rang out over the village every day for the next eight weeks as the men went down through the rock itself. Only one man at a time could work in the dark funnel and the pick axe handle had had to be shortened by half so that it could be swung in the narrow space. All the men of the Naam group had worked in rotation, each one being hauled out after an hour, smeared in dusty sweat, covered in mud and cut by the chips of flying rock.

After five weeks, the anxiety of the village had increased. Everyone had gone about telling everyone else that of course the water was there and that it could only be a matter of a few days at the most. But by now the clanging of the pick on rock sounded dead and thin as if it were coming from the distant hills. Gradually in the days that followed, the sound of digging began later and later as more and more water was pulled up by the roped buckets. Soon, several hours were spent emptying the well before lowering the first man down with the smooth handled pick. Finally, eight weeks after the digging had begun, came the day when more than a hundred buckets full of water were taken out without lowering the level of the water. The men gathered at the top of the well and shook hands.

A year later, Hamade had told her that a pump was coming for the well, though she had not totally believed it until the day it had filled the first jar. The well itself had saved hours of fetching and carrying. Now the pump saves more hours of lowering and hauling.

Joining her daughters and exchanging smiles with the

youngest wife, she looks down at the old way; the smooth white log still laid across the dark mouth of the well, the five or six rope-grooves at different depths, the frayed piece of rope still knotted around the wire handle of the sewn inner tube which served as a bucket for the long haul. That same bucket used to have to be hauled up fifty or more times to fill the seven jars, depending upon how quick you were and how much of the water was still left in the leaky rubber bucket when it reached the daylight.

At first, the new pump itself had attracted all the attention, making the drawing of water quicker and easier and keeping the well water cleaner. But soon the women had come to value the plain cement platform and walls as much as the pump itself. It is dangeously slippery when it gets wet, but it keeps animals away from the water used for drinking and washing; it makes the area easy to swill out and keep clean; it keeps litter and dirt and animal droppings from getting into the well itself, especially in heavy rains like last night; and it channels water down the drain to the open cement trough where animals can drink alone. At the well itself, the pump has just filled the last of the large earthenware jars.*

The carriers of grain and the carriers of water are headed in opposite directions. The youngest wife, conscious that she might be being watched, carefully shakes some water out of the jar so that it is not brim-full. Deftly she lifts it forward onto the edge of her bent left knee, gripping it by the rim while her right hand quickly wipes

---

* In response to the problems of finding a pump which is inexpensive, easily maintained, and strong enough to withstand continuous community use, UNICEF and the Government of India have worked together in recent years to develop the India Mark II hand pump. Over 100,000 India Mark IIs are now in use in the villages of India itself and the first field trials for Africa were conducted in Upper Volta. This pump is one of many now in operation in West Africa.

the mud from the bottom of the jar and adjusts the coiled scarf on the head. Then, in one movement both hands lift the 15 kilo jar into the air as the body moves under it and the knees and back straighten before the arms fall down to the sides and the youngest wife moves away, eyes levelled on the entrance of the village. Assita too moves on, smiling to herself and mentioning to her daughter to stop looking down at the path.

The struggle of the sesuka is often a calm, unhurried struggle with its moments of peace and pleasure, walking across the countryside, taking in its familiar sights and sounds, noticing small changes, falling in with a companion on the way. In good time, Assita transfers the calabash of grain to her hip so that she can bow her head in acknowledgement of an elder coming in the opposite direction along the path. He looks straight ahead but raises his flat palm in acknowledgement, a pair of traditional iron pliers hanging round his neck in case of thorns.

It was in this direction that Assita used to walk with her daughters, the baby wrapped tightly to her back, collecting guava and baobab leaves, sorrell and tamarind, sticky wizened grapes which they used instead of sugar, and the thick yellow cherries which are so delicious that they never lasted until they got back. On the way, she had taught the two girls how to recognise each plant and tree, told them how each was cooked and used, made collections to be taken back for the kitchens. Here they had learnt that the neere was never touched for firewood because its seeds bring high prices, that tamarind is as good as salt in millet porridge, that the seeds of the kulbūndu flower growing by the path are used for collecting dust and dirt in the eyes, that it is from the shiny brown karite seeds that their butter comes and their cooking oil and their soap, and that it is karite wax mixed in with the mud that makes the floor of their hut easy to swill and clean. Gradually each part of the landscape, each plant and bush and tree, had become a part of their lives as they began to see it through educated eyes. Now, there is little left to pick along a path that has been much used since the building of the mill.

Ahead of Assita on the path now is one of the few boys in Samitaba to have been sent to the primary school in the town. There he lodges with his father's sister, only returning to the village in the holidays. For the last few weeks he had been waiting at home to see whether he had passed the examination to go to the secondary school. Passing meant going to the town, learning French and science, maybe going on to the university in Ouagadougou, perhaps even one day going to Paris. It had been known, and all of these thoughts had gone through his head as the weeks went by. Failure, on the other hand, meant staying in Samitaba to work in the fields, or migrating to the town to try his luck wherever he could find it. Because of his long absences, and his education, he is not really accepted into the community of village boys. But the boy himself is quiet and respectful and his mother and father are well liked in Samitaba. And the whole village had quietly hoped with them. When the day had come for the list of successful candidates to be pinned on the notice-board outside the office of the Prefet, the boy had left at dawn to walk into the town. And all those who had seen him go had turned to their neighbours to confide in them the purpose of his journey. It must have been late morning when the boy had finally walked up the few wooden steps to the verandah which runs across the front of the Prefet's office. With tight jaws he had approached the white paper pinned among the duplicated appointments notices and yellowing government circulars. From inside the half-open doors had come the slow clack of a typewriter and the official sound of a ceiling fan. But his name had not been on the list.

Late that afternoon he had walked back into his village with many eyes on him. He had had the journey to prepare himself but it had not been easy. Later that evening one of the elders, a brother of the chief, had come to the compound to tell his father that he had watched the boy come through the village and go directly to his father's hut and that he had carried the burden in his mind like a man.

As Assita approaches now, the boy is talking to a much older youth sitting astride a motorbike. It is a young man who has returned from Abidjan for the planting but who is known for his scorn of the village and its ways. To the disapproval of the elders, he doesn't eat and sleep in the village, preferring to ride into the small town to eat in bars with other young men who are also back from the Ivory Coast for the season. As she passes, he is deriding Upper Volta's capital city for its few cars, poor roads and low buildings. Even before the harvest, the youth will be gone and eventually the day will come when he will no longer return even for the planting. As she passes, Assita suspects that a new ambition is growing already in his young listener as he feeds on the casually offered details of life in Abidjan and runs his eyes over the gleaming Yamaha with the traditional Mossi knife bound by leather thongs to the front forks.

The timing of Assita's approach to the place where two beaten earth tracks converge into the broad path to the mill is such that she cannot avoid falling into step with the woman now coming along the other path. Greetings are exchanged and Assita explains that her young son is not ill but merely sleeping at her mother-in-law's house. Her new companion is a large woman dressed in a faded purple fupoko and carrying a brightly patterned enamel bowl on her head-scarf. Assita glances sideways at the large silver hoops of the earrings, thin and hard against the fleshy, elaborately-scarred face. It is the face of the traditional healer, the one whose business it is to know how to extract the different properties of plants and herbs; which leaves and seeds and barks to boil for measles, diarrhoeas, or whooping coughs; how to use the Neere seeds to take away stomach pains, munmuka bark to treat kwashiorkor, kaga nuts to cure meningitis; how to make laxatives from the tamarind tree, haemorrhoid treatments from the bark of the kagdaga, strength-giving drinks with the beak of calao; how to select the white stones, medical woods and the bones of birds to make the threaded waist-beads and necklaces which ease childbirth and help infants to walk and grow strong teeth. Just as important, she knows the times and the seasons at which leaves must be picked, knows what words must be spoken and at what places offerings of salt must be made to the trees, rituals which give potency to the plants and profitability to the profession, secrets which she will pass on not to her daughter, who will one day leave the village, but to the daughter-in-law who will one day come to stay.

Now, Assita is complemented effusively on how well her daughters are growing up and asked, tactfully, if her son is walking yet. By the side of the path, lizards scuttle away at their approach and the brilliant electric-winged jay launches itself from a bare tree.

Many years ago Assita was also initiated and circumcised by this same woman who had led her, as a child of twelve, to a secret place out in the savannah. Like the other girls, she had had no inkling that the expedition was for any other purpose than the presentation of a belt of beads. But on arrival older women had held her down by her arms and legs, naked over a block of wood. So that her screams would not alarm the other girls waiting nearby, she had been told that her mother would die within twelve months if she cried out as the small sharp iron blade slices through her clitoris into the wood.

Then this woman's perspiring face had looked up into her own. And now they walk together side-by-side in the warm afternoon sunlight, talking about their children as they carry the white grains to the mill.

After the 'ko toogo', the time of 'bitter water' their wounds had been bathed twice a day, and the days of 'sweet water' had begun. The days of congratulations and ointments, praise and encouragement, stories and teachings, good food and lessening pain. And after the final jumping over the fires through the thick smoke in their white dresses, they had returned to the village, to her mother's embrace, to all the respect and status of adult womanhood.

Ahead of them walk the two girls. Three more years. Perhaps four. And Assita feels again the separation of perception, the oneness of a flowing stream divided into channels which lead only to stagnant pools of doubt, the unresolved struggle whose outcome is already decided. There is no decision to be made. If Assita does not do her duty then one day her daughters will simply disappear, taken by Hamade's mother to the camp of the initiation. And she would be right. No family, no husband, would accept an uncircumcised girl. It is not because there is a debate or choice that Assita has worked through the issue

94

so many times in her mind. It is because it is a way of coming to terms, of quietening powerful instincts, of giving shape to the chaos which is sometimes provoked in her mind, of teasing advantage out of inevitability.

For Assita herself it had been two weeks in which the axes of fear and pain and hardship in her life had been ritually redrawn in order to prepare her for adulthood, putting for ever into perspective the sufferings and the pleasures of all that had gone before, all that had happened since, and all that might happen in the future. It had been the attempt of her elders to prepare and fortify her mind against the hardship and fear which is never far from life in the village and from which the only relief is likely to be the fortitude of one's own mind. And as the women walk gently to the mill surrounded by the peace of the freshened countryside, Assita's thoughts cloud with morbid remembrances and imaginings for her children. She thinks of an infant, unattended for just a moment, crawling towards the open fire where the millet water boils, a wound accidentally made by the daba in a daughter's foot, the bad tooth which will eventually have to be taken out with the blade of a knife. Gradually her mind wanders through all the dark and sudden possibilities, even going back to memories of her own village and the girl whose hips were not yet big enough to give birth and who was in labour for three days, with the baby already dead inside her, and who finally died herself in the cart, at night, as in desperation they tried to take her into town.

Looking at her daughters, carrying the calabashes on their heads, she also wonders if the time will come again when there is no grain to be taken for milling, a time when they will have to carry on without enough to eat and drink, a time of such hunger and thirst that they will be glad to have water however filthy or food however poor.

95

And as she looks at them her mind turns to the girls who went through the initiation at her side, remembering them by the names they took for those two weeks, names which have never been used since except among that same group. And as she sees their names and faces, she thinks of the bond that was forged between them, the times when she has called or been called by the names known only to them, the occasions when she has given or been given support in times of trouble by that same group of friends who could never refuse their help. All of them she could count on with her life. And as her mind fills again with all that might lie in front of her daughters, and the fortitude and support which she herself has needed in her life and which they might need in theirs, she knows that when the time comes she will send them for their belt of beads. And she is easier in her mind.

Gradually the coughing of the diesel engine has been getting louder and now, as Assita and her companion walk into the clearing, they see the mill itself. Around the mud-brick building with its exhaust pipe thudding dirty air into the sky, several other women, most with young children, are already waiting. One of them is Azeto Ouedraogo, the president of the women's Naam group in the village, whose smile of welcome for Assita dies as she recognises her companion.

The traditional healer pretends not to have noticed as she leans over the walled lower part of the entrance to the millhouse and put her cloth-covered bowl on the concrete floor. To Assita's relief she announces that she will call back for the flour as she has to attend someone who has asked for her in one of the other villages which uses the mill.

Assita and the two girls place their own grain in the queue of calabashes on the mill floor. On the top of the doorway, set into the mud-faced wall, is the stencilled sign, 'NAAM-UNICEF'. On the open door itself, a government poster announces, in the languages of Dagara, Fulfulde, Kasena, Gulmacema, and her own Moore, 'If you can read, teach. If you can't, learn'. Inside, in the semi-darkness, the unfamiliar smell of hot oil and the unnaturally mechanical rhythm of the clicking pistons and the thumping exhaust cloak the seated figure of the miller. Behind him, the ribbed drum of diesel oil feeds the bottle-green engine. In front, the feeding funnel and the hammering chamber span the horizons of his day. As long as there are customers, he will sit here pouring the slightly dampened grains into the wide blue funnel above, filtering the falling sorghum or millet with his fingers as it travels down the metal shute, watching the quiet grey flour flow softly into the enamel bowl by his feet. Conscientiously, he keeps one hand in the shute itself, his fingers both controlling the flow and making sure that no coins, sometimes placed on top of the grain itself when it is brought by children, have accidentally been left there to fall into the grinding chamber. It is towards the end of the day, and a fine veil of white powder covers the miller's hair and clothes and spreads its train over the concrete floor of the mill.

For a long time, Assita had been anxious about depending on the mill. For the first two years she had regarded the grinding stones in the compound as her reality and the mill as her transient good-fortune. It would have been foolish to accept, glibly, that one of the most frequent of her jobs, the hardest and the longest, had been replaced by a walk along the footpath to the mill twice a week. But now the mill has been here almost three years and only for one day has it been out of action. Through the Naam meetings she knows that the small fee which the people of three villages pay to have their grain milled here is more than enough to pay for the fuel, the repairs, and the miller's wages. In fact it has been announced that the profits from this and ten other mills in the region are now enough to buy another mill for another group of villages. And so gradually she has come to accept the savings of time, and the savings of tiredness. In the wet season, it means that she spends more time in the fields, planting and weeding and conserving the grain and vegetables. In the long dry months, it has meant more time for collecting the ingredients and preparing the more nutritious sauces to go with the basic sagbo, more time to earn money by spinning cotton, sewing blanket pieces together, and making shia butter to sell in the market; more time to wean her son than she had for either of her daughters, to boil water and try to keep clean the weaning food saved from the main meals so that she can feed him more frequently; more time to make or alter clothes for the children, to resurface the floor of the hut, to water the trees in the plantation, to help build the new dam, to attend the meetings of the Naam. And Assita smiles to herself as she thinks how her mother-in-law always says that the flour doesn't taste the same.

Outside, she joins Azeto on the bench under the shelter, a thinly thatched roof on four poles, where she is teasingly congratulated on her new friendship with the traditional healer. One of Azeto's jobs as the leader of the women's Naam in the village is the dispensing of basic medicines and first aid from the new medical box*, and despite all the talk at meetings about traditional and modern health care going hand-in-hand, there is little love lost between their respective exponents in the village.

Soon the two friends are deep in conversation. At their feet, Assita's daughters have started a game of warè, thoughtfully picking up strategic pebbles from the twelve scooped hollows in the wooden board kept at the mill. Eventually a third woman arrives, pulling at her waist to untie a large red knot which holds a small baby low on her back.

For Assita, these discussions are one of the greatest benefits of the grinding mill, and one of the most looked forward to times of the week. Sometimes the two women talk of the rains and the crops and the granaries, or of the Naam group and its plans, or of the buying and selling prices of raw cotton and woven blankets. More often, the substance of their conversation is drawn from mother-hood, from the wellbeing and health of their families. Apart from the few classes she has been to herself, Azeto also gleans occasional information from other women's Naam leaders in the nearby villages. And increasingly, in the sharing of experience and problems, in the expression of doubts and anxieties, in the giving out of information and opinion, their conversations pursue the different strands in the twisted rope of tension between the old established ways and new untried ideas.

If they talk about pregnancy, then there is a tension

*The medical box at Samitaba, as in other villages of Yatenga, was given to the federation of Naam groups by the World Council of Churches. The WCC also pays the salary of a full-time Naam worker whose job it is to give classes to women's Naam members responsible for the medical boxes and to advise the Naam groups on health and nutrition matters. The training of this advisor, and some of the basic drugs, were provided by UNICEF.

99

between the new suggestion of a little more good food and a little more rest each day and the old way which forbids a pregnant woman to eat eggs or chicken or nuts and expects her workload to continue almost unchanged until labour begins. If it is the birth itself they are discussing, then both of them have heard that the midwife's hands should be washed with soap, that the cord should be cut with the boiled blade of a sharp knife, and that the wound should be wiped with alcohol and covered with clean cloths. But when Assita is delivered in the middle of the dry season, she knows that the cord will be cut with a razor blade, that the wound on the baby's stomach will be covered with medicinal herbs and that she could not possibly ask the traditional birth attendant to wash her hands. If it is a question of labour, then she hopes that she will again be lucky and have an easy birth. If not, if the labour is long and difficult, then she will be given sesame seeds and a drink made with the skin of cola nut. After that, there may be a glass of water in which her husband's belt has been soaked. If the labour continues to be difficult it will mean that the baby is not her husband's and will not be born until she confesses the real father's name.

If they are discussing breast-feeding, then Azeto has been told that babies should be put to the breast from birth because the yellowish fluid which comes in the first few days helps to protect the baby against disease. In practice, Assita knows that her new-born child will be taken away and fed on wegda — sorrel juice and water from the well — for the first three days, or given to another breast-feeding woman in the village, until all the yellow fluid, said to be dirty milk, has gone from her own breasts and only the white milk flows.

If it is weaning they talk about then strictly speaking a baby should not be given anything but breast-milk until the age of two. Some now say that the infant will not grow properly unless other food is also given from half way through the baby's first year. And at whatever time weaning does begin, tradition says that eggs and beans should not be given to a young child. On the other hand, the woman who came to talk to the village Naam group about weaning said that eggs and beans are exactly what is needed.

If one of their children is ill, then the different ideas of what to do are also in conflict more often than not. Traditionally, a child with measles should be given neither milk nor meat nor eggs. Others say that good things to eat will help the recovery. If a child has diarrhoea, the usual treatment is to stop feeding altogether or to use only the fruit of the baobab tree*. At the classes, Azeto is almost certain that they were told to continue breast-feeding a baby with diarrhoea. Or when meningitis and whooping cough spread quickly through families in the dry days of February and March, tradition says they are brought by the colder winds and so it is better for everyone to sleep indoors; while the new view says that the two diseases spread so quickly because so many people sleep close together in the small huts to keep warm in the cool night winds.

If their conversation turns, as it sometimes does, to the question of the initiation and the circumcision, then tradition is insistent on its necessity. But it is also sometimes said, and now widely believed in private, that it is the circumcision which leads to the frequent infections and causes many of the complications in childbirth, including the easy tearing of the tissues. And if they

---

*The fruit of the boabab contains calcium, vitamin C, tannin, sugar and mineral salts, making it a good absorbent and a helpful treatment for childhood diarrhoea.

discuss the age at which they hope their daughters will marry, one way says that a girl is ready to have a family at thirteen or fourteen and the other way says that she is not.

Assita grips the plastic bangle on her wrist as she shakes her head in response to something that Azeto is now saying. On the floor, the girls too are deep in concentration over the sophisticated tactics of wáré, staring at the arrangement of the pebbles in the different hollows of the board, trying to decide which pebbles can be safely moved and to where.

Sometimes, their discussions help the two women in coming to a decision. After talking it through with Azeto, who had given her the confidence, Assita began weaning her two-year old son after only four or five months, though she had continued to breast-feed him until only a month or two ago. She used boiled water when she could, fed him often and enriched the thin porridge with peanut paste, or beans or sometimes an egg. It was a big change. A talk by a visitor to the women's Naam group, an educated Mossi woman who was sent by the Union of village Naams, convinced her that the new way of weaning was right. But what made it possible was the fact that, like all wives, Assita has her own kitchen area and her own small plot of land outside the village hall. Even now, if she is not satisfied with what her own children have eaten at the communal family meal in the evening, cooked by each of the wives in turn, then she will afterwards take them into her own kitchen and prepare something extra for them from her own stock.

More often, the discussions of the two women are circumscribed by lack of information or by the lack of any way of knowing whether the pieces of information they have and the ideas they have heard about are valid and trustworthy. And sometimes their conversations become

102

desultory, enervated by the cutting of the cord between thought and action, by the lack of freedom to do much about the conclusions they might otherwise come to. If it were a conflict between different treatments or methods then eventually information and advice might be accumulated and a decision taken. But both women know that traditions are not medical treatments or opinions. They are part of their society, part of its morality, its religion, its culture. They are parts of the inter-locking jigsaw from which one piece cannot be taken out, changed in shape and pattern, and simply reinserted back into the picture of their lives.

This too brings in the horizons of action almost close enough to touch. Assita has thought often recently about the time six months from now, in the middle of the dry season, when she will give birth to a child. Of all the things she has heard about, things which some say ought to be done at the time of her delivery, there is only one that is within her power to do anything about. She will make sure that she has a clean sheet to put on the floor.

This afternoon Azeto is more optimistic. Perhaps it is because she has a little more scope for action that her thoughts find it easier to breathe. Being chosen as the spokeswoman for the forty-two women in the village Naam has given her some small purchase on the community. And being the person responsible for the Nivaquin has probably given her more. With the rains come the mosquitoes, breeding on stagnant pools. And from June to October, malaria invariably travels across Yatenga. No other illness kills as many infants in the villages of Upper Volta. And even among the adults, the disease saps the strength at the very time when it is needed in the fields. But in the last two rains, Nivaquin tablets have been available from Azeto Ouedraogo. Six cents buys five months' treatment — half a tablet a week — for an infant. Ten cents is enough to protect an older child. Assita now has to move up to the 25 cents for the three tablets a week which is the dose for a pregnant woman. With the money, Azeto gets into town and restocks the medical box. And there is no longer any argument in the village about the effect. Malaria, the most important disease in the country, is both less common and less severe than it was.

This afternoon, Azeto has been saying that she would like to do more than sell tablets. But two weeks training are not enough to do much. In theory, she can refer people to the medical centre in the town. In practice, two hours walk to the centre ends in more hours of queuing to see the one male nurse who has to get through two hundred patients a day and is well known for his short-temper.

More realistically, there is the possibility of organising vaccinations for all the children in the village. The immunisation team will come — and they will need to come three times over a year — if on each occasion they can be sure to find all the women with all their children in the same place at the same time. Confident in the Naam group, Azeto has committed herself to organising the attendance if the team will come. But only to Assita has she confided her idea of somehow starting some kind of village health centre right here under the shade, outside the mill itself, where most of the women frequently come with their children anyway, and where most of them have to wait as the two friends are waiting now.

On the floor at their feet, one of the twins is busy pounding a piece of shale into a flour of red powder on the hard earth. 'Can I borrow some salt?' asks her sister, pretending to arrive at her door. 'No you can't', she is told, 'go to your mother's house for a change, no-one lends me anything when I run out'. A small boy crawls towards them seeking entry into the game and crying to attract the girls' attention. 'Be quiet', says the other twin, 'I'll give you my breast in just a minute'.

Assita and Azeto are listening now to the shy young woman. Her first baby, a boy, is six months old and she too has been wondering what to do about weaning. As Assita advises her, the baby begins to try to suck at the mother's breast through her yellow T-shirt. Automatically, his mother lifts the shirt and offers the breast. But by now the baby has decided against it, turns away and tries to focus his large clear eyes on the noise of the mill. His skin shines with health and his body is sleekly rounded. But, almost inevitably, as infancy comes to an end and childhood begins, his shining health will fade. Around the shelter and the mill, children of all ages sit or play. Most have the swollen bellies of bilharzia, ascariasis, or hookworm. Many have the umbilical hernia of a stomach wall which has never properly healed since birth. Many also are under-weight for their ages and have sores at the edges of their mouth. Others sit on the ground without playing, listless and dulled, not even bothering to brush the flies from their eyelids, their bodies trying to defend weight and growth by reducing the expenditure of energy.

Almost unnoticed, an elderly woman, bent by a lifetime of bending, approaches the group. She pauses for a moment, listening to Assita, her own troubled breathing audible under the shelter. Her eyes, in a face as weathered and lined as the ancient village mortar, are alive with concentration as she bends towards the group. 'Only these, only these' she says, suddenly taking hold of the empty skin of her own breasts. The women pause respectfully. After a silence in which only her own breathing and the insensitive thud of the diesel engine can be heard, she explains to the younger women that only breast milk is to

105

be given until the child is two and that it is forbidden for a woman to have sexual relations with her husband during that time. More kindly, she explains that she has lived a long time, that she has seen it often before, that if another baby comes within two years then they will have to send the first child back.

A silence follows her unequivocal pronouncements as the elder's eyes question theirs. And in the silence, the woman moves on. From the opposite direction a small boy, sent by the miller, comes to tell the two women that their flour is ready.

The way which leads from the mill via the dam and the cart-track is a slightly longer way home for both Assita and Azeto, but it allows the two women to walk most of the way together, and the two girls to go for a swim. Covering the flour carefully with cloths tucked in around the rim of the bowls, the group gradually leaves the clearing and takes the downward path for the dam.

As they leave the sound of the diesel engine behind, Azeto mentions that the miller, a young man who lives in Somniaga, is gradually going deaf. For two hours after the end of each working day, ordinary conversation is lost on him. Azeto had asked about it today, but his only reply had been that he was very happy with the job.

Long ago, it had been thought that the miller might be a woman. After all, the mill reduces the amount of physical strength required to grind the grain. And it is a job which has been the sole preserve of women across the centuries. But now there is machinery and money and prestige involved, and so there were a thousand reasons why a woman could not be a miller. Instead, it was decided that women should participate fully in the running of the mill. Indeed they were placed in the majority of six to two on the Naam committee which manages the mill's operations. The two women smile to each other as they recall this decision. In practice, the two men participate in the machinery and the money and the women participate in sweeping and cleaning the millhouse and keeping it free of dust. No, not quite true, says Azeto. It was the women who suggested that the wàrè board should be kept at the mill and that the lower part of the doorway should be bricked in with a low wall so that they could relax as they waited without worrying about children playing near the machine.

THE cart on which Hamade has ridden into town stands empty outside a plain cement building. Cycles and iron-handled carts are cluttered around the half shuttered entrance. It is getting on in the afternoon and across the clearing comes the distant sound of a heavy pestle.

Hamade has just entered the building. From a small office, almost lost in the dark interior of the warehouse, the manager emerges. The two men shake hands. Gradually, as the eyes become accustomed to the dark, plump hessian sacks appear against the walls. Each contains 100 kilos of grain.

The brief formalities concluded, Hamade drags one of the sacks, heavier than himself, across the smooth concrete floor to the sliding doors of the hangar. It will be an hour before his neighbour finishes his business in the town. So Hamade sits down on the sack in the shade just inside the doorway. The air is cool in the warehouse, and all around him is the dry sweet smell of sacking and grain.

The warehouse in which he sits is not a shop. It is a security stock, built and managed by the Federation of Naam groups from surrounding villages. And its purpose is to lend grain to farmers whose own granaries have run out before the harvest. Hamade could have sold sheep or goats to buy the grain in the market, as he has done before and may need to again. But because so many villagers are forced to sell during the sesuka, the price of a goat falls and the price of a sack of grain rises. If he then tries to restock his herd after the harvest he finds that the terms of trade in the market place have swung drastically the other way. Hamade might also have borrowed money from a cousin in the same town. There would have been no interest to pay, only a small gift of a bowl of eggs or a parcel of shea butter when the loan was repaid. But if he takes the borrowed money to the market during the sesuka, a sack of grain costs $24. After the harvest, if he returns to the market to sell some of his grain and repay the loan, the price is $15 a sack.

Here at the Naam warehouse, he can borrow at least one sack of grain and repay it in kind, after the harvest, with one 100 kilo sack plus one 15 kilo tin. He does not need to sell animals or borrow money, he is neither exploited nor humiliated, and his debts are repaid with grain grown by his own hands.

Those same hands, along with many others from the surrounding villages, built the grain store. The materials, the girders and galvanised tin for the roof, the cement for the floor and walls, and the initial stocks of 200 sacks of grain, came from UNICEF, The World Council of

Churches, and other organisations co-operating with six 'Six S'* here in Yatenga.

The manager of the store emerges from the office again and sits on an old iron weighing scale opposite Hamade. He too has heard about a well which collapsed in the night's rains. The two men nod in agreement: earth wells are easier to dig but they never last as long as wells dug through rock. Hamade asks how many sacks of grain are left this season and the manager takes a rough guess before taking out a folded piece of lined note paper from his shirt pocket.

In theory, the one tin of grain 'interest' charged on each sack loaned out is meant to enlarge the stock and expand the service to more farmers. In practice, the grain bank, like almost everything else in Yatenga, depends upon the rain. In year one of operations, all of the initial 200 sacks were lent out to farmers during the sesuka. After the harvest, 200 sacks and 200 tins were returned. No one defaulted. That made it possible to lend out 230 sacks in year two. But in that year the rains faltered and the harvest fell. Everyone who had borrowed grain was asked to pay back at least the interest — one fifteen kilo tin. But only 163 out of the 220 had returned the sack itself. The rest were allowed to postpone repayment for a year. That meant that in year three there were only 197 sacks available to be lent out. None went to those who already

---

*'Six S' — Se Servir de la Saison Sèche en Savane et au Sahel — is the international organisation which was formed after the drought of the early 1970s with the aim of supporting rehabilitation and development in the Sahel. Much of the material aid to the Naam groups in Yatenga comes via 'Six S' whose director, Bernard Ledea Ouedraogo, is also the founder of the modern Naam movement. Six S is a consortium of the Swiss government, Misereor, Action de Carem, Comité Catholique de la Lutte contre La Faim et pour le Developpement, Cebema, and the Conseil Cooperatif du Quebec. UNICEF and the World Council of Churches aid the Naams directly.

owed grain from the previous year. The rains fell, the harvest was good, and all of the 197 sacks came back with interest. Some of the previous year's debts were also repaid and the security stock crept back to over 200 sacks. Of those, 146 have already been lent out, including the one that Hamade is sitting on.

Both men know the limitations of this security stock. It is too small. And it is not expanding in the way that was hoped. Both also know that although it helps the farmers to survive the sesuka without being exploited, the bank itself does not solve the basic problem of how to increase production. And without any increase in production, the bank's position in Yatenga is as precarious as the soil itself.

Hamade gets up to follow the manager to the back of the warehouse. Behind the wall of grain sacks, a platoon of new ploughs are marshalled together in the dim light. Hamade grips the perforated handles of green painted iron. Just in front of his feet, the heavy naked steel prow rests on the conrete floor. Above it, green chains dangle, waiting to be attached to ox or donkey. 'Bourguillon',Drome, France, suitable for use in all soils' says the oval label on the flat iron shafts, though the manager confides in Hamade that the ploughs are made in Ouagadougou. This time next week, the dozen ploughs waiting here will be being hauled through the earth, turning the soil under the hands of Naam members. An hour walking behind a plough will turn over at least five times as much land as an hour spent wielding a daba. So hoeing takes less time, or less people, or covers more land. Just as important, the ploughs can help to compensate in the years of cruel rains. If the rains fall in huge downpours followed by weeks without even a shower, then the immature crops wither in the fields and the planting has to be done all over again — as many as three or even four times if the rains are particularly heartless. When that happens, the season is so foreshortened that there may only be time to prepare and plant a few of the fields . . . unless there is a plough.

This year in Samitaba the fields will again be dug by dabas. But the Samitaba Naam group has also applied to the Federation of Naams for two ploughs of the same kind as the one now under Hamade's hands on the floor of the warehouse. International organisations, including UNICEF, have given the ploughs to the Federation. But the Federation does not give them to the villages. Their cost must be repaid — with interest — by selling a part of the increased production which the plough itself makes possible. That way the Federation can keep on supplying more ploughs to more villages. The Samitaba Naam has estimated that it will be able to pay back the cost of the two ploughs in only one year. . . if it rains. But they will have to wait. Other Naams in other villages have been waiting longer.

Reluctantly leaving the plough, Hamade follows the dim figure further back into the recesses of the warehouse. It is the two pumps that the store manager wants Hamade to look at this afternoon. Pulling back a tarpaulin, he reveals one of the two mobile diesel engines, a Briggs and Stratton, made in Milwaukee, USA. As he picks up a rag from a bowl of reddish water and begins to clean the mud off the engine housing, the manager explains that the two motor pumps have been brought here for storing during the wet months. When the rain ends in October, they will again be towed into the vegetable fields of the Naam groups of Titao.

Hamade has seen the Titao fields, surrounded by a wire fence like the plantation and with the same 'Naam — UNICEF' notice hanging at the corner. Each year, when the harvest is over and the dry season begins, these two engines start up by the edge of the lake behind the dam, pumping water through steel pipes into cement tanks placed at strategic points around the fenced two hectares of the market garden. With the water, the Naam members have work and incomes in the dry season, growing onions, salad, potatoes, cabbages, tomatoes, carrots, even tobacco, to improve their diets, earn money, and avoid migrating to the Ivory Coast for wages.

Hamade is more than usually curious about the fields of Titao. For now there is also, a dam at Samitaba, where a small lake has already formed after the night's rains. The manager, who deals with people from all the surrounding Naams, is a clearing house for news as well as grain. Picking up another rag, Hamade starts on the far side of the engine housing.

Fifteen tons of vegetables were taken from the Titao fields in last year's dry season, according to the manager, and that doesn't include the stocks which the Naam members grew for their own use. Eighty families worked there. Eighty husbands didn't have to migrate for the dry season. And those who really put time into it earned between $200 and $300 in cash. Ten of the young men, he reports, even bought bikes with their share at the end of the season. Everybody put a fixed part of their earnings back into the Naam funds to repay the cost of the motor pumps, irrigation pipes, cement for the water tanks, and the 500 metres of wire fencing. With the money, the Federation of Naams plans to launch another market garden next year on the edge of the same lake*. The spin-off has already

*What the warehouse manager does not know is that two days earlier on the 7th June 1982, it had been announced in Paris that the French franc was being devalued by 7%. The announcement followed a de facto decline in the franc's value which amounted to a real devaluation of about 25%. The West African

112

started, says the manager, pointing to three or four dozen bare-metal watering cans stacked against the far wall of the warehouse. Local artisans have found a good market in Naam members who want something to help them take water the short distance from the cement tanks to their crops.

Hundreds more people have applied for 'dry season' land in Titao than can be accommodated. More pumps and more fencing are needed and expansion is slow. But with their earnings, the Naam members who work in the Titao fields have another way of growing enough to get through the sesuka. And they also eat better throughout the year. Thinking that maybe he could report back on all this to the Samitaba Naam, Hamade thinks of the questions they will ask as he scrapes mud from the red paintwork of the pump. Yes, the land does of course belong to other families who farm it as usual in the rains. But they loan it at no charge to the Naam groups during the dry season. They are glad to let it be used as the roots of the vegetables enrich the soil and stop it blowing away in the long months without rain. And yes, it is easy to sell the vegetables. They are bought by the URCOMAYA state owned co-operative and transported South to Ouagadougou. Some are even sold abroad.

Hearing his name called, Hamade sees the dark silhouette of his neighbour against the bright oblong entrance to the warehouse. With a damp handshake he takes his leave of the manager, and begins to heave the sack towards the waiting cart.

---

franc is pegged to the French franc at the rate of 50 CFA to IFF. Set against the still broader context of a steadily rising US dollar, the effective cost to the village Naam groups of a Briggs and Stratton diesel motor pump has risen by 50% in little more than a year.

In the clearing on the outskirts of the small town, the meeting has slowly been assembling for the last hour. First to arrive were the younger men, although they automatically gathered toward the two ends of the line of rough wooden benches, leaving the centre, close up against the fat trunk of baobab tree, for the elders to sit under the densest shade. Already, Bernard Ledea Ouedraogo, the founder of the modern Naam movement, has arrived and is sitting on a small table, swinging his legs. He is a stocky, powerful looking man in his late forties, dressed in a round-necked tunic, a lighter colour than the earth, and loose baggy trousers. Last week, his brown leather casual shoes were walking the streets of Geneva as he attended the meetings of 'Six S', the international organisation of which he is the director and which is the main source of outside aid to the Naam groups. But today those shoes are covered with the dried mud of Yatenga on the first day of the rains.

Now some of the elders themselves are beginning to arrive, moving slowly to seat themselves under the baobab, hands resting in the laps of their white cotton robes which reach almost to the loose sandals made of old tyres or strips of worn leather. Some wear the traditional pugla, others the conical straw hats, shaped with leather-covered wooden ribs, which shade the whole of the face. It was one of the elders who suggested the meeting. For there has been some tension between the Naam movement and the government's own rural development organisation.

A few local government officials have also taken their seats, to one side of the line of benches and, behind them, the Naam representatives are gradually coming in, leaving carts and bicycles in the broken shade behind the tree. Some of the men know each other from other meetings but many formal introductions are being made, hands shaken, news exchanged, as they wait for the meeting to begin. From the village of Ingare comes the youth chairman of the Naam groups in the region, fluorescent shirt tucked into his working trousers, the deep lines on his face bunched up together as he smiles and shakes hands all round. His own Naam group is called 'Yamatarba', meaning 'intelligent improvement'. In the finely crocheted cap, the treasurer of the Watinoma Naam group, a name meaning 'come our village is good', has also arrived from Yensẽ. Shaking hands with him now is the representative from Kallo, wearing flared green trousers and an old blue woollen ski cap. The name of his Naam group is 'Metba', or 'hands together to build'.

Hamade and the leader of the Samitaba Naam are the next to arrive, shaking hands with old friends from other villages and being introduced to new-comers. Greeting them now is the Naam president from a far-off village on Upper Volta's borders with Mali. He is visiting relations nearby and taking the opportunity to meet other members of the Naam movement. Hamade has heard of the man's village, famous for a well so deep that it is the only village in Yatenga, perhaps even in the whole of Africa, where the water is drawn by the men. As they talk, Bernard Ledea Ouedraogo himself joins them to shake hands. He tells the visitor that he has been to his village and asks if the well is still giving good water.

Soon the informal conviviality is interrupted by the call to order and Hamade retires to sit on the end of one of the benches.

After the introductions, Bernard rises to explain why the new Naam idea has spread through the villages. Between his phrases, he inserts the soft 'ce' sound to lend flow and rhythm to his speech, a habit for which the Mossi of Yatenga are known as the 'Yadce' Mossi.

Bernard himself grew up in a village like other boys, swam in rivers like them, herded goats like them, was initiated and circumcised like them. Only an accident separated his life from theirs. One day, in a burst of colonial enthusiasm for educating, Bernard and the eighty other boys who happened to be in their compounds when the visitors arrived, was enrolled in a primary school. For the other eighty, school ended a few years later. For Bernard, it ended with a doctorate from the Sorbonne.

In the clearing now, Bernard is talking about the time when he worked as director of the Young Farmer's Federation, trying to improve life in the countryside. It was here, he is saying, that he first saw the imported ways failing, saw the village committees die for lack of interest, saw the idea of European-style co-operatives not understood or enthused about, saw the loans go unrepaid, the plans not carried through, the development efforts stagnate.

At these words, Hamade can see the elders under the tree nodding their agreement and exchanging words. Incongruously, a goat with a black patch over one eye wanders into the meeting. There is only one green thing on the beaten earth floor of the clearing, a twig with a few leaves left on it, and the goat has come for it. Soon driven off by a hail of stones from the younger men, it wanders over to chew at some vegetables poking out of the panier of a motorbike.

Now Bernard is describing how he had begun again to study the traditional ways in which the Mossi got things done, the ways of the Sôngtaaba and the Sosoaga and the Kombi Naam, describing the responsibilities and titles of the chosen officials: the Kombi-Naaba, who was responsible for the youth of the village, sometimes called the Mogho-Naaba among the Yatenga Mossi; the Toogo-

Naaba, who was responsible for the techniques and the timing of the work; the Sor-Naaba, responsible for everything to do with travel; the Basi-Naaba who was the disciplinarian, empowered to prosecute any wrong behaviour from lateness at work to irreverance towards the elderly; the Tilb-Naaba, his opposite, who had the uncontestable power to forgive and to pardon; the Maan M-Yam-Naaba, responsible for entertainment, for pleasure, and for publicly satirising those who are lazy or those who drank too much 'dolo'; the Lemb-Naaba, responsible for tasting all food which was to be eaten by the community as a whole during the festival for the Naam; the Rasâmb-Naaba who tried to anticipate and solve the minor problems which always arise between boys and girls in adolescence.

Bernard is into his rhythm now and as he speaks every muscle in his face is eloquent, every vein in the thick-set neck, every line of the forehead, every turn of the waist, every raised finger as he brings out the compelling rhythm of the language, repeating its verbal formulas, voice rising with rhetorical questions and falling with the answers, appealing to the elders for support on the traditional things and to the local government officials for agreement when his drift moves closer to them.

Now he is asking if the young respected the elders in the old days. Without waiting for an answer, he asks 'what about today?' Were the taboos observed in your young days? But what about today? Would a man ever have made love to a woman on the floor? But what about today? If you are my friend is our relationship not holy? But what about today? Would a man who was a Mossi ever tell a lie even if tortured to death? But what about today? Wasn't that part of all that the elders taught to us in stories during our childhood, that a man does not tell a lie? But what about today? If in the old days you were having a siesta and a man came and knocked at your door would you ever say to him 'go away, I am sleeping?' But what about today? And so it goes on, question, answer, pause, the murmurs of approval, the catalogues of old and new.

For the elders, it is a long time since they heard anyone speak like this, a long time since they heard anyone with youth, vigour, authority, anyone who has lived in the world of 'les blancs', speak with respect for the traditions, with pride in Mossi culture, with confidence in a Mossi future.

At the edge of the group, Hamade looks across to the group of elders. One very old man is asleep against the tree in the heat. But the others seem almost rejuvenated by what is being said. And he can almost physically feel the savouring of the words by the elders as they nod their heads and keep their eyes fixed straight ahead not looking, as they often do, as if they are living in a world of their own.

Several of them are slowly nodding in approval. For to them. Bernard seems to realise that growing old should be an upward as well as a downward path. For the slackening of the muscles and the decline in strength, for the loss of teeth and hair and beauty, for the increase in pains and illness, and for the sadness of failed ambitions and narrowing choices, for the realisation of time past grown long and time future grown short, for all of this there ought to be a counterbalance in society, a growing in status and influence, in the place you have earned in your family, in the respect in which you are held by the community. But only in the old Mossi ways is there this social counter-weight to the physical progressions of life. In the new world of money and change, a world which only wants to pay the wages of the young and strong, a world which reserves its status and respect for those who can read and repair motor-bikes, a world which is organised to exacerbate rather than offset the mental and physical sadnesses of age, the elders must decline in influence and usefulness and their status fall through respect to tolerance and finally to resentment.

Now Bernard is describing, for the benefit of the younger government officials, the traditional structures, the philosophy and the taboos, the different mentalities of the different tribes and villages, the political and legal systems of the Mossi, the tools and methods of cultivation, the systems of trade and money, and the values enshrined in their beliefs. From the compound, a small boy runs out with a straw hat for one of the elders.

Bernard turns to his growing belief that it was on these foundations, not on the hollow shells of imported ideas, that the future of the Mossi could be built. And of all the traditional structures, it had seemed to him that the Naam was the way of the future. As a microcosm of the Mossi way, and of Mossi political organisations, with its participation by all for the benefit of all, the adaptation of the Naam idea to the development of the Mossi had seemed to him to be worth suggesting to the villagers of Yatenga.

Here, he tells the story of the encouragement received from others; from Ahmed Mostefaoui, now UNICEF Regional Director for West and Central Africa based in Abidjan, who gave him moral support to leave his government job and found the new Naam movement and material support when he had done so; and from Stanislas Adotevi, now UNICEF's Resident Programme Officer in Upper Volta, who secured for him a year's bursary from the Canadian International Development Research Centre to study and collect ideas from the villages and write up his experiences. To more nodding from the elders, he describes how the people knew immediately what he was talking about when he went into the villages and talked of the Naam. Even one or two of the government employees are now beginning to nod in agreement and some have taken felt-tip pens from the pockets of their white shirts and are making the occasional note.

Behind the benches, Hamade can hear the sounds of women and children, some of them working even at this moment in the 'Kin Naam', the 'come in and work' which the women organise informally in the afternoons to enjoy each other's company while they work at spinning cotton. The raw cotton is bought from travelling merchants and spun, in spare moments, onto spindles twirled through fingers dusted with the fine ash from the fire. Round the compound wall, against which the chrome yellow flowers of the Tevetia tree glow in the afternoon sun, comes a small boy kicking an old battery box along the ground. He approaches the edge of the meeting and is shooed away.

Meanwhile, Bernard is explaining that seven hundred and thirty seven Naam groups have been formed across Yatenga, organised on the traditional lines of Mossi democracy, and united in Federations and a Union of Naams. Aid comes, he tells them, from people whose land the villagers have never visited, people who have never been to Yatenga, people the Mossi have never met, but who have heard of the drought and of what has been happening in the Sahel. If the load you have to carry is too heavy to lift onto your head, he reminds them, then it is right to be glad of the hand that helps you. But a Mossi must always use two hands of his own.

The aim of the new Naam, he announces quietly, is not to be an organisation dependent on aid. Its aim is to regenerate the Mossi people themselves in Yatenga and beyond. Bernard has quietened his audience now and is speaking with a slow seriousness. A man dies twice in his

120

life, he is saying. He dies when his enthusiasm dies, and he dies when his body dies. That is the danger for the Mossi, the danger that the erosion of their own ways by foreign ways, their own values by foreign values, will destroy their enthusaism for grappling with life, their sense of responsibility for solving their own and their community's problems. This is the first and the only important death. That is one of the reasons why the village Naams have to organise and work for two, three, sometimes up to ten years years before they receive any outside aid at all. Because the aid is only useful if the will is there.

Hamade smiles to himself as he thinks of the new dam at Samitaba. But Bernard has turned to appeal to the local government officers now, the representatives of the Organisation Regionale pour le Developpement, asking them not to resent the Naam groups or discriminate against their members, asking for their support and co-operation. Drawing on the stock of approval which he has built up amongst the elders, he begins to speak of the changes which will have to be made, the new methods and the new technologies which will have to be applied, the support that will be needed from the government and the ORD, the bad things about traditional ways which will have to be discarded and the good things about the ways of Europeans which ought to be adopted. The Mossi have neglected economic development, he suggests, and they are going to have to live in the real world of money and interest rates and trade and inflation. Now he is drawing the nods of agreement from the young officials. He is near the end of his address now and he steps back once more to face the elders.

Materialism will not take hold of our people, he asserts. We will go forward from traditional society not in the direction of 'les blancs' but in a new way, a Mossi way, to create a new development and a new Mossi society. Applause rings out around the clearing as young and old join in approval, the elders now feeling able to accommodate and sanction the changes which they know in their heart of hearts are necessary but which usually spring from a philosophy which undermines their lives, negates what they have worked for, suffered for, lived for through so many years.

Sitting next to Hamade, staring at the ground, is a young man who arrived half an hour ago on a motor bike. On his knee is a copy of 'Confidences', the true-love confessions magazine from France. A digital wrist-watch with an expanding metal bracelet hangs slackly round his wrist, his denim shirt tucked into tight flared trousers which fall short of his bare feet. Cigarette smoke curls from his nose as he looks down. And Hamade feels, also, for his pain.

The meeting is thrown open for questions now and Hamade prepares to leave as he knows his neighbour is anxious to get back. As he stands and moves round the back of the benches where the carts and bicycles have been left, he pauses a moment to hear what one of the elders has risen to say. It is not a question he is asking. It is a statement to the effect that he agrees with what Bernard has said about Mossi ways and Mossi values but what he wants to say is that not all today's young people are disrespectful to the traditional ways and values. With pointed arm the elder singles out a young man who is sitting at the back of the meeting.

It is a young man who has recently returned from Abidjan. He has returned for the planting as a young man should, says the elder, and he returned on a new motor-bike, bought with his earnings from many months of work on the coffee estates. But when he saw that his father did not have enough grain in his granary for the sesuka,

122

when he saw that money and food were short in his household, he rode away one morning on his motor-bike. That evening, he came back on an ordinary pedal bike with a large sum of money for his father. There is silence for a moment as heads turn, and then the meeting breaks into prolonged applause. The young man covers his face with his hands and lowers his head to his knees. At the front, Bernard nods his head slowly, his lips pursed.

O N the path under the wall of the dam, Assita walks alone as the light begins to fail. Her daughters are already bathing near the edge of the lake and Azeto has just set off on the path around the edge of the small lake to her own compound. Looking up at the great bank of boulders, purple in the evening light, Assita remembers how the men had to be shamed into building the dam of which they are now so proud. No one knows how many stones are in the wall of the dam, perhaps more than 20,000 each just big enough to be carried on a woman's head.

Before the dam, water had run down from the hills after the rains and a stream had flowed through the shallow valley. In the days following the downpour, the stream would dwindle to a trickle and finally stagnate in pools which slowly disappeared to leave only muddy depressions in the land. But whether it had flowed on to the South or sunk down into the earth, the water had passed uselessly by Samitaba. Meanwhile, buckets had to be drawn by hand to water the animals, animals which stayed in the village, mooching by the wells, bringing parasites and dirt and disease to the compounds as they mixed with the water that was used for drinking and cooking. In the dry season, when the water had disappeared entirely from the wells themselves, tins and jars had to be fetched from four kilometres away. And even in the rains, the well remained deep because the water flowed away in the rivers before it had the time to sink through the compacted earth, percolate through the porous rocks, and replenish the ground waters of Yatenga. Meanwhile, the rains from the hills flowed by.

Building a dam across the course of the stream had been postponed as often as it had been discussed. But finally, in the dry season of two years ago, the women's Naam of Samitaba had met and announced that, if the men would not build a dam to hold the rains, then the women would begin to build it themselves. It had not been a bluff, but it had worked anyway. Over the long months of the dry season, the Naam groups of Samitaba and three other nearby villages had organised the four kilometre trek to the distant hills, arranged for food to be brought out, and for troubadours to beat the time. Even the children of seven or eight years old had carried back the smaller rocks, walking in a line behind the adults carrying the heavier stones.

After a year, the question of the Samitaba dam had been brought up at a meeting between 'Six S' and the Federation of Naam groups in the nearby town. There, it was decided that the three village Naams had proved themselves. A week later, the ten-ton truck, one of the few in the whole of Yatenga, had lumbered down the shale road to the half built dam. A crowd had gathered round the huge vehicle as the driver and his assistants swung open the high cabin doors, marked with the blue emblem of UNICEF, and began to undo the chains on the tailboard. On the back were shovels and picks, carts for towing stones, bags of high resistance Portland cement from Abidjan for the facing wall, and the two motor pumps from

124

Titao to be used for pumping water to mix the cement. Unloaded, the truck had been guided across the open land of hard shale towards the hills, carrying the men. On its return, carrying over 500 rocks, it had found the rest of the Naam members waiting to unload the stones onto carts to tow them into position on the dam.

Assita comes to the end of the path under the great bank of silent stones and turns towards the village. For most of the year there will be a lake here behind the dam. The cattle will water themselves and the village will be a cleaner and healthier place. For Assita, this alone would have been reward enough.

For two years after the dam was built, the level of the water in the village wells themselves did not change. But now the talk in the surrounding villages is that the water is rising in the wells again and that the season when there is no water at all is getting shorter because the dam is holding the water until it sinks through the earth.

Eventually, as the dry season wears on, the wells will again go dry. But, for a while at least, the water stays behind in the dam. Hoisted out in buckets and filtered through fine cloth, it loses much of the reddish-colour which gradually increases as the level of the lake falls. In the end, even the lake disappears, and the struggle for water is as it always was.

But when, after months of nothing but dust and parched colours, the rains finally fall and a lake forms behind the dam, it is as if their labours have been miraculously performed all over again. The women come to wash their clothes here, or walk back this way from the mill, or just stroll by its edge for a few minutes in the early evening. Quickly, 'going to the dam too much' has become village parlance for laziness.

For a few more moments, Assita waits by the lake for

125

her daughters. The hard white sun has glared all day on Yatenga and she is glad to rest her eyes on the water. The sky is turning through purple now as evening falls. Over the surface of the lake, a special silence seems to carry each sound separately, as if it were something distinct and precious in itself. And as she waits, she hears even the faint snap of a swallow's beak as it takes an insect low over the water.

On the road some distance away, Assita sees a cart passing slowly by. Recognising the silhouetted figure of Hamade, she moves to walk towards the roadside thinking to ride back with him the rest of the way. Then she remembers that he will almost certainly have a sack of grain with him on the cart and decides to let him go back alone.

Brittle laughter comes from the direction of the village now and Assita looks across the slope to see the figures of boys lighting handfuls of straw as they surround the ancient termite hill. Tonight, the termite flies which fill the air in ephemeral thousands a few hours after the rains, will add variety to the meals in some of the compounds. As she approaches up the slight slope, the boys are closing in on the termite hills, buildings without architecture, which line the pathway to Samitaba. Fatally attracted by the light of the burning straw, the termites fly into the flames and fall in their hundreds as their wings frizzle. On the ground, eager hands scoop their insect bodies into waiting bowls. Back in the village, there will be laughter soon as the boys try their hand at winnowing, pouring the insects from a great height for the slight wind to blow away their singed wings. Then their mothers will do the cooking, stirring them in an iron pot, knowing that they will make the children sick unless they are roasted until thoroughly dry.

Entering the village, Assita and her daughters become

conscious of their hunger as the smell of cooking comes from all quarters. Tonight, in their own compound, she has more than a suspicion that there will be chicken to celebrate the rains.

LATER THAT NIGHT, after the evening meal, lying awake in her own hut with the very last of the evening light just visible, a halo around the rush door, Assita resolves that tomorrow will be the day to visit her husband's aunt with the news. Sleep is coming now and the aches in her body are almost pleasant. At her side, her small son turns over in his sleep. The child ate well tonight and she was pleased that Hamade had taken some notice of him. He had even given him some pieces of white meat. She had been right about the chicken. Two had been killed and cooked by the eldest wife. Hamade had seemed cheerful and said something about vegetables and seeing men with hands cut by the wire they were making into fences. They had all watched as the breast and the legs and wings were given to the men and the elders. Suddenly, she remembers that she has forgotten to put the guinea fowl eggs into the hens' nests. It will have to be done tomorrow if there are to be more chickens. Guinea fowl are such bad brooders. The neck and the feet and the innards had been given to the children while the women had sucked at the bones and drunk a little of the water in which the carcase had been boiled. When the guinea fowl hatch she will have to remember to take the chicks from the hens straight-away. Then they will have to be fed on chillies and water for a while. It's time the hens eggs hatched too. Tomor-

127

row she will put them into the big clay jar with the holes in it, the one she used to use for steaming until it got cracked. None of the pots seem to last as long as they did. Then the eggs can be put inside on the soft bed of old cotton seeds pulled out at the spinning. The heat will be sure to hatch them again. Very softly, rain is beginning to fall in heavy drops on the thatch. Tomorrow she will go to her husband's aunt to tell her the news. Then there will be no more eggs for a while. . .

———————

Annexe

Statistics about children and world development drawn from the United Nations family:–

SOURCES

GNP..World Bank
Population..UN Statistical Office
Age Distribution ....UN Population Division
Life Expectancy......................................UN Population Division
Infant Mortality Rate........................ UN Population Division
Child Death Rate..World Bank
Primary Enrolment Ratio ....UNESCO
Adult Literacy Rate..UNESCO
Access to Safe Water..WHO
Per Capita Calorie Supply...FAO
Food Production ....FAO

	GNP Per Capita 1980 (US.$)	Population Mid-1980 (in mils.)	Percentage Under 15/ Under 5 1980 (%)	Life Expectancy 1980	Infant Mortality 1975-82	Child Death Rate 1980	Primary School Enrollment Ratio[a] Male/Female 1979	Adult Illiteracy Rate Male/Female 1980	% With Access to Safe Water 1975	Daily per Capita Calorie Supply as % of Requirement c) 1977	Average Index for Food Production 1978-1982 (1969-71=100)
World	2430	4,508	35/13	59	89	12	—	—	—	—	—
Low Income b) (Below $420 p.c.)	230	511	—	48	130	22	77/47	—	29	94	95
Mid-Income ($420-$4,500 p.c.)	1,400	1,139	—	60	80	11	100/93	—	50	107	108
Industrialized Market	10,320	714	—	74	11	1	100/100	—	—	131	111
Industrialized Non-market	4,640	353	—	71	25	1	95/96	—	—	137	109
AFRICA											
1 Algeria	1,870	19.6	47/19	56	125	19	100/83	40/77	77	97	80
2 Angola	470	7.3	44/18	42	160	34	—	—	—	93	82
3 Benin	310	3.6	46/19	47	160	34	78/42	57/93	21	100	99
4 Botswana	910	0.8	50/20	50	88	—	100/84	31/37	—	—	89
5 Burundi	200	4.3	44/18	42	127	25	28/18	61/93	—	99	99
6 Cameroon, U.R.	670	8.7	42/17	47	115	21	100/93	36/63	26	106	109
7 Cape Verde	300	0.3	36/11	61	87	—	—	46/66	—	—	—
8 Central African Republic	300	2.3	41/17	44	154	32	100/54	41/80	16	92	101
9 Chad	120	4.5	42/17	41	154	32	51/19	—	26	72	91
10 Comoros	300	0.4	43/16	47	97	—	—	—	—	—	—
11 Congo, People's Rep. of	900	1.6	43/18	59	135	27	100/100	—	17	99	79
12 Egypt	580	44.0	40/16	57	110	14	88/61	44/73	66	118	93
13 Equatorial Guinea	340[4]	0.4	42/17	47	49	—	—	—	—	—	—
14 Ethiopia	140	32.0	45/19	40	150	32	48/24	—	6	78	83
15 Gabon	3,680	0.6	33/13	45	122	—	—	—	—	—	97
16 Gambia	250	0.6	42/18	42	204	—	56/28	73/97	—	—	71
17 Ghana	420	12.1	47/19	49	107	19	80/62	40/63	36	85	82
18 Guinea	290	5.1	44/18	45	172	37	45/24	—	10	78	86
19 Guinea-Bissau	160	0.8	39/16	42	154	—	100/60	58/85	—	—	91
20 Ivory Coast	1,150	8.3	45/19	47	132	26	91/58	42/76	19	107	107
21 Kenya	420	17.1	50/21	55	92	15	100/94	36/65	17	96	86
22 Lesotho	420	1.4	41/16	51	120	23	84/100	42/19	17	95	91
23 Liberia	530	2.0	48/20	54	160	34	83/51	58/82	20	101	98
24 Libyan A.J.	8,640	3.1	46/20	56	107	13	100/100	23/64	100	122	139
25 Madagascar	350	9.0	44/18	47	76	11	10/87	—	26	111	95

#	Country											
26	Malawi	230	6.1	48/20	44	179	39	70/48	52/75	33	97	99
27	Mali	190	7.2	45/19	43	160	34	36/20	81/92	9	83	88
28	Mauritania	440	1.7	46/19	43	149	31	36/29	—	—	94	76
29	Mauritius	1060	1.0	34/12	65	38	2	99/99	15/28	—	—	91
30	Morocco	900	21.0	46/18	56	114	15	93/56	59/83	—	107	87
31	Mozambique	230	10.8	44/18	47	120	23	100/90	56/89	—	78	75
32	Niger	330	5.5	47/20	43	151	31	29/17	90/100	27	91	93
33	Nigeria	1,010	80.0	47/20	49	141	28	—	54/86	—	83	87
34	Rwanda	200	5.1	46/19	45	112	29	74/67	38/63	35	94	106
35	Senegal	450	5.8	45/18	43	153	32	51/34	69/86	37	95	89
36	Sierra Leone	287	3.6	44/18	47	215	50	45/30	—	—	85	86
37	Somalia	130³	4.9	44/19	44	150	32	64/36	90/100	33	88	84
38	South Africa	2,300	30.0	42/16	61	101	18	—	—	—	116	102
39	Sudan	410	18.9	44/18	46	131	22	60/43	62/86	46	96	102
40	Swaziland	680	0.6	45/18	47	140	—	100/100	30/42	—	—	114
41	Tanzania, U.R.	280	18.5	40/19	52	108	19	100/94	22/30³	39	87	92
42	Togo	410	2.7	45/19	47	115	21	10/85	53/82	16	92	81
43	Tunisia	1,310	6.5	42/15	60	107	10	100/85	39/66	70	115	120
44	Uganda	300	13.6	45/18	54	101	18	58/42	36/69	35	93	89
45	Upper Volta	210	7.1	45/18	39	219	51	26/15	82/95	25	93	95
46	Zaire	220	26.0¹	45/18	47	117	22	100/77	23/61	16	102	88
47	Zambia	560	6.0	47/20	49	111	20	100/89	21/42	42	90	96
48	Zimbabwe	630	7.6	47/19	56	79	12	100/96	22/36	—	109	97

ASIA

#	Country											
49	Afghanistan	170²	16.4	43/18	37	205	35	36/7	74/95	6	107	95
50	Bahrain	5,560	0.3	—	67	57	—	32/53	—	—	—	—
51	Bangladesh	130	90.0	46/18	46	140	20	79/49	50/81	53	—	94
52	Bhutan	80	1.3	42/16	44	156	23	15/7	—	—	90	105
53	Burma	170	36.0	41/16	54	107	13	87/81	—	17	103	99
54	China	290	1,008.0	32/10	64	49	5	100/100	—	—	103	116
55	Cyprus	3,560	0.6	26/9	73	20	—	—	—	—	—	99
56	Hong Kong	4,240	5.2	27/10	74	13	(-)	100/100	6/24	—	119	53
57	India	240	684.0	41/15	52	129	17	92/63	44/72	33	89	101
58	Indonesia	430	151.0	42/15	53	99	11	100/89	22/42	12	102	110
59	Iran	2,180⁴	39.0	45/18	59	115	14	100/82	44/70	51	122	112
60	Iraq	3,020	13.5	47/19	56	84	17	100/100	29/69	62	90	90
61	Israel	4,500	4.0	34/13	72	18	(-)	95/97	—	—	123	106
62	Japan	9,890	118.0	24/7	76	9	(-)	100/100	1/1	—	126	93
63	Jordan	1,420	3.4	46/18	61	75	6	100/99	24/52	61	62	89

		GNP Per Capita 1980 (US.$)	Popula- tion Mid-1980 (in mils.)	Percentage Under 15/ Under 5 1980 (%)	Life Expec- tancy 1980	Infant Mor- tality 1975-82	Child Death Rate 1980	Primary School Enrollment Ratio[a] Male/Female 1979	Adult Illiteracy Rate Male/Female 1980	% With Access to Safe Water 1975	Daily per Capita Calorie Supply as % of Requirement[c] 1977	Average Index for Food Production 1978-1982 (1969-71=100)
64	Kampuchea	70[4]	6.8	42/13	37	263	—	—	—	—	78	41
65	Korea, D.R.P.	1,130[2]	18.3	40/14	65	37	2	100/100	—	—	119	133
66	Korea, Rep.	1,520	38.0	34/12	65	37	2	100/100	4/12	71	117	130
67	Kuwait	19,830	1.5	47/21	70	30	1	100/96	28/49	89	—	—
68	Lao	90[4]	6.8	42/13	37	263	—	100/85	—	—	94	100
69	Lebanon	—	2.7	39/14	66	44	2	—	16/36	—	112	83
70	Malaysia	1,620	14.4	41/15	64	33	2	94/92	23/38	62	116	116
71	Maldives	260	0.2	—	47	—	—	—	18/18[4]	—	—	—
72	Mongolia	780[2]	1.7	43/16	64	59	4	100/100	—	—	106	97
73	Nepal	140	15.0	42/17	44	156	23	100/49	66/95	9	89	88
74	Oman	4,380	0.9	46/19	48	135	—	76/37[3]	—	—	—	—
75	Pakistan	300	85.0	47/19	50	131	18	81/31	61/82	29	99	101
76	Philippines	690	50.0	44/17	64	59	4	—	10/12	43	107	114
77	Qatar	25,080	0.2	—	58	57	—	—	—	—	—	—
78	Saudi Arabia	11,260	9.3	45/19	54	121	18	78/49	70/98	84	87	69
79	Singapore	4,430	24.0	29/10	72	13	1	100/100	11/30	100	135	147
80	Sri Lanka	270	15.0	36/12	66	48	3	89/81[4]	18/24	20	97	121
81	Syria	1,340	9.3	48/18	65	67	5	100/84	26/66	75	104	157
82	Thailand	670	48.0	43/16	63	59	4	85/78	7/17	22	97	128
83	Turkey	1,470	46.0	39/15	62	131	21	100/96	19/49	75	116	111
84	United Arab Emirates	26,850	0.8	—	63	57	3	—	70/81	—	—	—
85	Viet Nam	—	55.0	41/16	63	106	6	100/100	—	—	96	107
86	Yemen, A.R.	430	5.9	45/17	42	170	50	59/9	84/100	4	82	94
87	Yemen, P.D.R.	420	2.0	46/18	45	153	31	99/42	52/84	24	81	103
NORTH AMERICA												
88	Canada	10,130	24.0	23/8	74	12	(-)	100/100	—	—	127	109
89	United States	11,360	230.0	23/7	74	14	1	—	1/1	—	133	115
LATIN AMERICA												
90	Argentina	2,390	28.6	28/10	70	48	2	100/100	4/5	66	124	122
91	Bahamas	3,300	0.2	—	69	—	2	—	—	—	—	—
92	Barbados	3,040	0.3	28/9	71	27	1	100/100	2/2	—	—	84
93	Belize	1,080	0.2	—	—	—	—	—	—	—	—	—
94	Bolivia	570	5.9	44/17	50	138	25	87/76	21/42	34	87	106

95	Brazil	2,050	122.0	42/16	63	82	7	90/87	25/28	77	111	117
96	Chile	2,150	11.3	33/11	67	46	2	100/100	6/9	84	110	93
97	Colombia	1,180	29.0	40/15	63	59	4	100/100	14/16	64	98	122
98	Costa Rica	1,730	2.3	38/13	70	29	1	100/100	8/9	77	113	112
99	Cuba	1,410[2]	9.8	32/9	73	23	1	100/100	4/5[2]	–	118	105
100	Dominican Republic	1,160	5.4[1]	45/16	61	73	6	95/96	25/27	55	102	94
101	Ecuador	1,270	8.6	44/17	61	86	8	100/100	18/24	42	90	95
102	El Salvador	660	4.9	46/18	63	85	7	83/81	30/37	53	94	119
103	Grenada	1,080	7.5	44/17	59	79	6	74/63	41/57	40	92	112
104	Guyana	690	0.9	40/14	70	48	–	100/98	4/7	–	–	94
105	Haiti	270	5.1	44/17	53	121	18	–	67/76	14	92	92
106	Honduras	560	3.8	48/19	58	95	10	92/85	36/39	46	93	82
107	Jamaica	1,040	2.2	41/13	71	30	(–)	99/100	10/7	86	118	96
108	Mexico	2,090	71.0	45/18	65	60	4	100/100	13/19	62	113	103
109	Nicaragua	940	2.8	48/19	56	97	10	83/88	–	70	116	95
110	Panama	1,730	1.9	40/14	70	36	3	100/100	14/16	79	104	102
111	Paraguay	1,300	33.0	44/17	65	49	3	10/98	10/17	13	119	111
112	Peru	930	18.3	41/16	58	94	9	100/100	11/28	48	98	83
113	Suriname	2,840	0.4	51/17	68	39	–	100/100	32/37[3]	–	–	182
114	Trinidad & Tobago	4,370	1.2	33/10	72	30	1	90/97	–	–	103	85
115	Uruguay	2,810	2.9	27/9	71	42	2	100/100	5/5	84	105	97
116	Venezuela	3,630	14.3	42/16	67	45	2	100/100	16/21	–	102	102

EUROPE

117	Albania	840[2]	2.8	37/14	70	50	4	–	–	–	113	104
118	Austria	10,230	7.5	20/6	72	17	1	99/98	–	–	135	110
119	Belgium	12,180	9.9	20/6	73	13	(–)	100/100	1/1	–	141	107
120	Bulgaria	4,150	8.9	22/8	73	22	1	97/95	3/7	–	143	114
121	Czechoslovakia	5,820	15.3	24/9	71	19	1	92/93	–	–	139	115
122	Denmark	12,950	5.1	21/6	75	9	(–)	–	–	–	127	11
123	Finland	9,720	4.8	21/7	73	9	(–)	85/85	–	–	116	105
124	France	11,730	54.0	22/7	74	11	(–)	100/100	–	–	136	115
125	German D.R.	7,180	16.7	20/6	72	13	1	95/98	–	–	139	126
126	Germany, F.R.	13,590	62.0	19/5	73	15	1	–	–	–	127	110
127	Greece	4,380	9.7	23/7	74	20	1	100/100	4/16	–	135	122
128	Hungary	4,180	10.7	22/8	71	27	1	90/96	1/2	–	133	130
129	Iceland	11,330	0.2	27/9	76	9	1	–	–	–	–	109
130	Ireland	4,880	3.4	31/10	73	15	(–)	100/100	–	–	141	124
131	Italy	6,480	57.0	22/6	73	18	1	100/100	3/5	–	136	111
132	Luxembourg	14,510	0.4	18/6	72	13	1	97/98[3]	16/20	–	–	107
133	Malta	3,470	0.4	23/8	72	38	2	100/100[3]	–	–	–	133
134	Netherlands	14,470	14.2	22/6	75	10	(–)	100/100	–	–	125	127
135	Norway	12,650	4.1	22/6	75	9	(–)	99/100	1/2	–	119	114
136	Poland	3,900	36.0	24/9	72	23	1	–	–	–	140	102

	GNP Per Capita 1980 (US$)	Population Mid-1980 (in mils.)	Percentage Under 15/Under 5 1980 (%)	Life Expectancy 1980	Infant Mortality 1975-82	Child Death Rate 1980	Primary School Enrollment Ratio[a] Male/Female 1979	Adult Illiteracy Rate Male/Female 1980	% With Access to Safe Water 1975	Daily per Capita Calorie Supply as % of Requirement[c] 1977	Average Index for Food Production 1978-1982 (1969-71=100)
137 Portugal	2,370	9.9	26/9	71	38	2	100/100	14/24	65	127	78
138 Romania	2,340	23.0	27/9	71	31	2	98/98	2/5	–	130	145
139 Spain	5,400	38.0	26/8	73	15	(–)	100/100	4/9	–	127	127
140 Sweden	13,520	8.3	20/6	75	8	(–)	98/98	–	–	120	116
141 Switzerland	16,440	65.0	20/6	75	10	1	86/87	–	–	127	115
142 United Kingdom	7,920	56.0	21/6	73	14	1	100/100	–	–	133	118
143 Yugoslavia	2,620	23.0	24/8	70	35	2	99/98	6/19	–	136	115
144 USSR	4,550	268	24/9	71	29	1	–	1/2	–	136	108
OCEANIA											
145 Australia	9,820	14.9	20/8	74	13	(–)	100/100	–	–	127	123
146 Fiji	1,850	0.6	37/13	72	40	2	100/100[3]	12/23	–	–	99
147 New Zealand	7,090	3.1	27/9	73	14	1	100/100	–	–	124	105
148 Papua New Guinea	780	3.1	44/17	51	111	14	73/55	–	20	87	106
149 Samoa	650	0.2	–	68	–	–	–	–	–	–	–

Key

1) 1980
2) 1979
3) 1978
4) 1977
(–) Less than half the unit listed for child mortality
— Not available
a) These are *gross* enrollment ratios and do not exclude underage or overage children. When the ratio is greater than 100 (because of the inclusion of these children) the figure shown in the table is 100.
b) Excluding China and India
c) Aggregate national figures for daily per capita calorie supply can disguise undernutrition among the poorest sections of society.

Further information about UNICEF and its work may be obtained from UNICEF offices and National Committees for UNICEF

UNICEF Headquarters
United Nations, New York, New York 10017

UNICEF Office for Europe
Palais des Nations, CH 1211, Geneva 10, Switzerland

UNICEF Regional Office for East Africa
P.O. Box 44145, Nairobi, Kenya

UNICEF Regional Office for West Africa
B.P. 443, Abidjan 04, Ivory Coast

UNICEF Regional Office for the Americas
Casilla 13970, Santiago, Chile

UNICEF Regional Office for East Asia and Pakistan
P.O. Box 2-154, Bangkok, Thailand

UNICEF Regional Office for the Eastern
Mediterranean
P.O. Box 5902, Beirut, Lebanon

UNICEF Regional Office for South Central Asia
11 Jorbagh, New Delhi 110003, India

UNICEF Office for Australia and New Zealand
G.P.O. Box 4045, Sydney N.S.W. 2001, Australia

UNICEF Office for Tokyo
c/o United Nations Information Centre
22nd Floor, Shin Aoyama Building Nishikan
1-1, Minami—Aoyama 1-chome
Minato-ku, Tokyo 107, Japan

There are National Committees for UNICEF in the following countries:-

AUSTRALIA
AUSTRIA
BELGIUM
BULGARIA
CANADA
CZECHOSLOVAKIA
DENMARK
FINLAND
FRANCE
GERMAN DEMOCRATIC
 REPUBLIC
GERMANY, FEDERAL
 REPUBLIC OF
GREECE
HUNGARY
IRELAND
ISRAEL
ITALY
JAPAN
LUXEMBOURG
NETHERLANDS
NEW ZEALAND
NORWAY
POLAND
PORTUGAL
ROMANIA
SAN MARINO
SPAIN
SWEDEN
SWITZERLAND
TUNISIA
TURKEY
UNITED KINGDOM
UNITED STATES OF
 AMERICA
YUGOSLAVIA

Addresses may be obtained from your telephone directory.

UNICEF PUBLICATIONS

UNICEF NEWS is a quarterly magazine published in English, French, Spanish and German. Aimed at a general audience, it seeks to bring alive some of the key issues confronting individuals and organisations involved in social change in the developing world. Some articles are contributed by experts in their particular fields. Others are descriptive feature stories and profiles, drawing on the example of programmes, usually those in which there has been some UNICEF co-operation, to illustrate and dramatise change in action.

Assignment Children/Les Carnets de l'enfance is published twice a year in English and French. This review is for a specialised audience of those professionally engaged in social development and is intended as a working instrument which will keep them up to date with the latest thinking in areas of concern to mothers and children.

For subscription details, write to: UNICEF, Information Division, United Nations, New York, N.Y. 10017. USA or UNICEF Office for Europe, Information Division, Palais des Nations, 1211 Geneva 10, Switzerland, giving the title of the publication concerned.